FURNITURE MAKES THE ROOM

FURNITURE MAKES THE ROOM

+ **Create Special Pieces to Style a Home You Love**

+ **BARB BLAIR**
FOUNDER OF KNACK STUDIOS

PHOTOGRAPHS BY
PAIGE FRENCH

CHRONICLE BOOKS
SAN FRANCISCO

Library of Congress Cataloging-in-Publication Data:

Blair, Barb, author.
  Furniture makes the room / Barb Blair ; Photographs by Paige French.
    pages cm
1. Furniture painting. 2. Furniture finishing. 3. Interior decoration—Themes, motives. I. Title.

  TT199.4.B535 2016
  684.1—dc23

                           2015015943

ISBN 978-1-4521-3999-9

Manufactured in China

MIX
Paper from responsible sources
FSC
www.fsc.org   FSC™ C008047

Designed by Hillary Caudle
Typeset in Alright Sans, Eames Century Modern, and Letter Gothic

Arm-R-Seal by is a registered trademark of General Finishes Sales and Service Corp.; Behr paint is a registered trademark of Behr Process Corporation; Benjamin Moore paint is a registered trademark of Benjamin Moore & Co.; Citristrip is a registered trademark of W.M. Barr & Company, Inc.; Community Tap is a registered trademark of The Community Tap, Inc.; Cusco is a registered trademark of Carrosser Co. Ltd.; Etsy is a registered trademark of Etsy, Inc.; Fiddes Wax is a registered trademark of Fiddes & Sons, Ltd.; Fiestaware is a registered trademark of the Homer Laughlin China Company; Fire-King is a registered trademark of Anchor Hocking Glass Corporation; FrogTape Delicate Surface Tape, Multi-Surface Tape, and ShapeTape are registered trademarks of Shurtape Technologies; Instagram is a registered trademark of Instagram, LLC; Klean-Strip is a registered trademark of W.M. Barr & Company, Inc.; Minwax, Minwax Polycrylic, and Minwax Special Walnut Stain are registered trademarks of Sherwin-Williams Company; Miss Mustard Seeds is a registered trademark of Mustard Seed Interiors, LLC.; ModPodge is a registered trademark of Enterprise Paint Manufacturing Company; Montana Gold is a registered trademark of L&G Distribution.; Murphy Oil Soap is a registered trademark of the Colgate-Palmolive Company; Old-Fashioned Milk Paint is a registered trademark of The Old-Fashioned Milk Paint Co., Inc.; Pratt & Lambert is a registered trademark of Pratt & Lambert Inc. Corporation.; Purdy, Purdy China Brush Series brush, Purdy Nylox, and Purdy White Bristle Brush are registered trademarks of Purdy Corporation; Pyrex is a registered trademark of Corning Incorporated Corporation; Ralph Lauren is a registered trademark of PRL USA Holdings, Inc.; Spackle is a registered trademark of Muralo Company, Inc.; Stendig Calendar is a registered trademark of High Design LLC DBA; Titebond II Premium Wood Glue is a registered trademark of Franklin International, INC.; Zona is a registered trademark of Lakeside Collaborative, Inc.

10 9 8 7 6 5 4 3 2 1

Chronicle Books LLC
680 Second Street
San Francisco, California 94107
www.chroniclebooks.com

To my sweet family, Jon, Conley, and Brynn.

You are my everything.

CONTENTS

- **PART III** - - - - - - - - - - - - - - - - - -

When I consider my first memories of "home" and what helped shape my personal views of décor, I think back on my upbringing on the West Coast in a little town outside of San Francisco. The home I grew up in was definitely eclectic. My parents did missionary work overseas, so our home was full of treasures from their travels: carved wooden elephants and camels from India, and side tables made of cherry wood with bone inset designs of tigers, elephants, and trees. There was also the gorgeous writing desk that we still call "the Singapore desk" because it came all the way from Singapore (where I was born, by the way!), with its detailed carved scene of men pushing an oxen-pulled wagon up a hill. The pendulum clock of dark weathered wood with tarnished brass innards, and my mother's big oak table with the five extra leaves that we were always excited to extend for guests. (Years later, I serendipitously found one just like it at an antique store—it was my first big purchase as a married adult.) My mother had the gift of hospitality, and her table was always gorgeous but not fancy, because everything had been found and collected. Mom had a soft spot for Depression-era glassware in reds, greens, and yellows, and she collected vintage Fiesta ware, Pyrex, and Fire-King. My childhood home told the story of our family—what we experienced and valued, where we traveled, the people we encountered, and the beautiful tables we set for feasts with friends and family.

I learned from an early age that creating a home means filling it with things that you love. Home doesn't mean perfection—it means taking the time to collect and gather furniture and objects that you find beautiful and meaningful. I learned that the value in possessions lies solely in the value that we give them.

Now that I am grown and married with a family, my home tells its own story. You can find bits and pieces of my childhood home (like my own collection of vintage Fiesta ware and colorful Pyrex—go figure) among the newer cherished items: artwork created by my children; the picture of the clay cliffs on Martha's Vineyard where my husband and I stayed for our tenth anniversary; the artwork created by friends; favorite thrift store finds (like the signed print I bought for three dollars and later discovered was done by a famous German artist!); the little stone dinosaurs from a family cross-country trip; the antique picture of Robert E. Lee that my father-in-law used to salute every night before bed, which now hangs in our dining room, reminding us of his quirky personality; the piece of our old fence that my sister-in-law painted with the words "eat good food," now hanging in our kitchen; the tablecloth that we pull out every Thanksgiving—we write on it what we are thankful for, then safely tuck it away until the next year; the big wooden window frames on our den walls that I rescued from a garbage pile in Tennessee many years back; and painted furniture pieces in every room, each with

its own story of beauty and redemption. My home tells the story of my life, and if I were to walk you through its rooms, I would love sharing these tales with you.

What story does your home tell? What would I see, walking through its rooms? What treasures would come to life as you shared their stories with me? I hope to help you answer these questions and connect more deeply with the items in your home, and to show you how to bring intention into your space by choosing and creating furniture pieces that express your story. After all, home is about more than high-end designers and the latest trends—it's a place where we have total creative freedom and the "rules" are made only by us.

My deep connection with the concept of home is what inspired me to start my studio,

Knack, and it is why I have made furniture design my life's work. Rescuing a forlorn piece of furniture and turning it into a work of art is a way to bring soul into your décor. In these pages, I reveal the multiple functions that live within every piece of furniture and walk you through the process of unlocking the unique personality of the pieces you cherish. I hope you come away with a whole new outlook on furniture and how playing with different settings is a way to keep your home fluid, fresh, authentic, and alive.

The heart of this book is about creating a space you love and that reflects your life. You'll find that step one is understanding that furniture—and the meaning, colors, stories, and accents that come with it—is what truly makes a room.

PART I

+ **Getting Started**

In my first book, *Furniture Makeovers,* I cover everything you need to know about starting out in furniture design. It presents twenty-six basic techniques—from sanding and prep to adding paint, stains, and stripes—and has an extensive tools and resources section. I consider that book "Furniture 101." My goal with this book is to take you to the next level of furniture design, to go more deeply into the creative process and styling.

In this book, I've created fifteen brand-new pieces. All of the instructions for creating these designs can be found in the back of the book, along with a list of the necessary tools and materials. Additionally, I show you how to style the furniture in different home and room settings. I want to help you stretch your mind to take furniture beyond the expected functions in your home. The rooms photographed are in actual homes—beautiful, normal, everyday homes and studios that have been carefully curated and designed and are stellar examples of the philosophy of Knack: live with what you love! Moving the bright and colorful furniture from room to room in these environments allowed me to demonstrate the versatility of each piece and the uniqueness of each space. You'll soon be envisioning all sorts of new ideas for your home.

Furniture has so much personality and character—that is why I love working with it! Sometimes people have trouble immediately visualizing where to place the colorful furniture pieces that I create at Knack. When someone sees primary colors and immediately says, "That would be great in my nursery or teenager's room," I feel compelled to agree—but I gently suggest other options, too. All pieces work in all types of rooms! The same dresser that would look terrific in a kid's room can also bring a unique statement to your dining room, den, foyer, guest room, living room—any room in your home. Instead of being afraid of color, see it as a neutral base for everything else. When you mix colors with things that you have collected and love, a beautiful style story develops. Our homes tell a very clear story of who we are and what we hold dear, and unique, colorful furniture pieces are an important part of that story.

As you pick pieces for your home, consider the furniture's intended use as well as how it could best be used in your space. For instance, a chest of drawers is . . . well, a chest of drawers, but it can also be an entertainment center or a sideboard in a dining room. Learning to see pieces beyond their intended purposes opens up a whole new world of styling. *You* get to choose how a piece will be used. A gigantic Victorian sideboard does not have to be relegated to a fancy dining room. Visualize it as additional storage in a bedroom, a changing station in a nursery, or a place to store all of your cookbooks in the kitchen.

It's also important to be able to move things around. It's rewarding to go "furniture shopping" in your own home—just like "shopping" your closet for something to wear. When you get the itch to redecorate, grab that coffee table from the den and put it at the foot of your bed, loaded down with soft blankets and your favorite books, or take the desk you have been using in your teenager's room and turn it into a dining room side bar full of glasses, linens, and tonics. When you make intentional choices in choosing functional and artful furniture pieces, you'll never have the thought, "Where would I put that?" Instead, when you see a piece you love, you'll immediately think, "I can't wait to build a room around this piece" or "I will find a home for this piece because I love it!"

Sometimes I discover a gem and immediately know it will be a statement piece when I get through with it. Other times, I dream up a design in my head before I have even found a piece of furniture, and it doesn't come to life until I stumble upon just the right piece. Remember, there is no need to rush into a furniture buying decision. Take the time to look around and pick a good quality piece, a piece that you are in love with. All furniture has character and personality, so pick the one that really speaks to you.

When I choose a piece of furniture, it is usually because a detail or form stands out to me. I tend to be a sucker for curves and detailed carvings—all characteristics of the 1940s. It's funny—in all the years I've been painting, it wasn't until I started writing this book that I was able to pinpoint this preference. I just always picked what I liked, and over time a pattern emerged. The same could be true for you. Pick what you're naturally drawn to, because these are the pieces you will want to live with and style around for a long time. Beyond that gut feeling, there are some additional things to consider when choosing furniture for your makeover projects:

Structural condition. Think about how the furniture will be used in your space. First and foremost, is the piece structurally sound? Or will it need repairs before it is functional? If so, can you do those repairs yourself, or will you need to pay for carpentry? Be sure to factor in the cost of repairs before deciding if something is the right investment. Make sure all of the drawers work properly and that there is enough storage for your needs.

Style. What is the style of the piece? Is it rustic, modern, art deco? Will this piece fit into the décor of your home? I mean *fit*, not *match*. One of my favorite things to do is to mix modern and eclectic styles together. The juxtaposition creates a fun, lived-in atmosphere. But your personal style is of course up to you. What do you want to convey when you design and display this piece? Perhaps a particular era of furniture design appeals to you. Consider the storage space and usage of the piece, and if that will suit the needs of your home.

Odor. This may seem silly, but it's important! Make sure that the furniture is free of unwanted smells. Strong smells of mildew or smoke are really difficult, if not impossible, to get out, so consider this before you purchase a piece. No one wants their clothes or linens to smell bad, but unfortunately they will if they are stored in a piece of furniture that has a strong odor. Wood is porous, and it absorbs smells over time, making them hard to remove. Trust me—I've fallen in love with a piece and had to break my own heart by not buying it because of the strong smell of smoke. It just isn't worth it in the end.

Is it solid wood? You can paint any type of surface, especially with all of the paints on the market these days, but I am a fan of solid wood. Typically, solid wood furniture is the highest quality. Solid wood can be stripped and sanded, whereas other materials, like veneers (unless it is a wood veneer) or particle board cannot. That's not to say that you can't paint that vintage resin veneer piece, because you can. I just feel that if there is a solid wood option, you will be happier with your investment in the end.

Now, you aren't going to refinish and paint every piece of furniture in your home. So as you search for furniture, also look for basic pieces that you will leave "as is" to mix in with the more designed pieces. You want balance. I liken it to denim in fashion. It is always good to have basics that can work with everything and be dressed up or dressed down. For instance, my dining room table is a massive walnut pedestal table with five leaves. Among your designed pieces, incorporate the warmth of wood grain to round out the space.

PLANNING YOUR DESIGNS

When it comes to designing furniture, the word *intention* comes to mind. When I acquire a piece, sometimes I know what I will do with it immediately; other times I need to sit with it for a while before a design plan forms. I am not in a hurry. For me, designing furniture has never been about cranking it out, designing what I think others might like, or what the retail market is asking for. Of course I pay attention to current market trends and what my customers like, but ultimately these factors do not dictate my creative process. I approach furniture just as any artist creates—inspired by the season of life that I am in, the colors of nature around me, my travels, and things I'm drawn to in the fashion and art world. Good design doesn't always happen immediately, so take your time and bring intention to every design decision you make.

FUNCTION

When you have found a piece that you like, think of how it will live and function in your home. Will it function for its intended purpose (a dresser as a dresser) or will you give it new purpose (a dresser as a media cabinet)? This will likely affect how you approach the design. What colors are in the room where you'll place the piece? What fabrics? Patterns? Textures? Are you starting the room from scratch and making this the focal piece? (My favorite option!) Or does it need to complement an existing room design? Ask yourself these questions until you have a clear direction in which you want to take this design.

INSPIRATION

When starting a project, I like to create a secret board on Pinterest. I find my inspiration for furniture design in many things, but never in other furniture! For instance, one board may feature photos of mountain ranges, a paint-flecked shirt, a piece of artwork, and a baby fox

for the spectacular color of his burnt orange fur. Another may show lots of different eggs painted gold as inspiration for a design using gold leaf. I gather images that inspire me in both color and texture, and from there my color palette, paper, and hardware choices start to emerge.

CHOOSING DETAILS

Paint colors, hardware, and beautiful gift wrap and wallpapers—there is so much fun to be had in choosing each special design element for your furniture piece. It is important to make thoughtful choices about every little detail. Use that amazing roll of vintage wallpaper you scored at the Goodwill for a few bucks, or go all out and pick an extravagant wallpaper to splurge on. Whatever is going to make your furniture design achieve your vision, go for it. Trust me; you will not regret it.

SKETCH

Once I have the piece, an inspiration board, and a plan for the colors and details in my head, I sketch out the design on graph paper with colored pencils. I do this because it is a challenge for me (as a self-taught artist) but also so I can put my vision on paper and see the elements come together before actually getting started. It is exciting to see a design that has existed only in your mind come to life on paper. I believe it's crucial to be able to clearly see your designs before executing them. You do not need to be a master artist to create a colorful inspiration sketch. I myself am completely untrained, but using lined graph paper and a ruler gives me guidelines and a place to start.

Don't be intimidated. As you sketch, you may notice something you hadn't thought of or an element you can tweak and improve. Graph paper works well because the lines and boxes provide guidance and make it a little easier to get a clean sketch, but you can use any type of paper.

I don't worry about drawing a piece to scale—that's not the purpose of my sketches. It's about making sure the details and color palettes shine.

I love to get out my watercolors and define my palette by adding pretty watercolor circles to my sketch. The palette then guides me in the paint choices I make. I find it is so much easier to create a beautifully executed piece when all of the details and design elements are thought out before I begin hands-on work on the piece. By the time you are done sketching and gathering paint colors, papers, and hardware for your project, you have a clear direction and, more important, confidence in what you are about to embark on. This is key.

Now, a warning—and one I've given hundreds of times before. Do not be that person who simply slaps paint on a piece of furniture to fill a void in a room or to satisfy a quick fix. It will come back to haunt you, and you will end up wanting to change your design, but since you were completely uninspired on the first go-round you will be even less inspired now to start over. (Which, by the way, will take twice as much work!) Instead, spend the time at the outset to be intentional about every aspect of your design. Use these steps to guide you through the creation of your very own masterpiece: a masterpiece that commands attention and completely *makes* the room that it calls home. You will thank me for it later!

PART II +

+ The
Designs

CASSIOPEIA

GOLD-FLECKED SIDE TABLE

I purchased this side table as part of a bedroom set from a woman who was moving. I loved the whole set because each piece was flat and straight, with modern lines and details. It was the perfect blank canvas for trying a new technique.

My inspiration for using this technique was a white-and-gold-flecked shirt I found online. Isn't that crazy? Inspiration comes from many different places, and I could not wait to try my hand at some paint splatters on furniture. I chose liquid gold leaf for the flecks because I wanted the final result to resemble a starry sky.

The beautiful and rich dark gray background is the perfect backdrop for the golden flecks, and the piece absolutely glows in the morning and evening light. The stars and galaxies inspired me to name her for a constellation: Cassiopeia. To finish the piece, I added a pretty glass knob that has its own flecks within and a beautiful geometric paper drawer liner that also reminds me of star formations.

Simple unexpected displays, such as
these spools of vintage ribbon, bring
personality to what would otherwise be
a purely functional piece.

IN THE FOYER

While it may not be the first spot you think of, a little side table fits
perfectly in a foyer or entrance. This particular piece has a drawer and
two shelves, great for organizing and storing all of the things you need
to set down on your way in the door (and pick back up on your way out!).
The handmade platter on top holds keys and phones, and the hook on
the wall above works for hanging your bags. The drawer is a convenient
place to stash takeout menus, stationery, journals, and magazines, while
the shelves act as a mini style vignette, housing favorite spools of ribbon
and treasured books. Artwork on the wall and a tiny stool that adds extra
surface space finish off this look nicely.

An ever-changing display of treasured items finds its way into the cubbies of this piece. Carefully edited, but still personal.

24

IN THE BEDROOM

A bit more predictably, the side table also works great beside the bed as a nightstand, perfect for holding bedtime reading and a morning cup of coffee. The drawer provides storage for bedtime necessities such as lip balm, lotion, tissues, and journals, while the shelves provide ample room to display books and collections. The glamour of the gold flecks pairs beautifully with the white refurbished headboard and bedding in this calming room. The piece comes to life when flanked by original artwork by an emerging artist, a colorful wool kilim rug, a found stool, and industrial lighting. A room always feels considered when it has a healthy dose of wood, glass, and metal. In this case, the color of the kilim brings the neutrals to life, while the industrial lighting and found metal and wood add an element of grit.

You can never go wrong with bold black-and-white artwork! The eye-catching hawk piece in this bedroom complements the glamorous gold of the nightstand.

CASSIOPEIA / Gold-Flecked Side Table

What you choose to collect and display
in your house gives your visitors clues
to who you are.   27

IN THE LIVING ROOM

The side table simply glows next to this Victorian couch. The styles of the pieces are different, but they work wonderfully together. The very straight and modern lines of the side table are softened by the graceful and wild curves of the sofa. The gold flecks pick up the rich color of the couch, and their shine can be seen throughout the room. Mixing styles and eras is one of my favorite things to do. Distinctive, unexpected looks emerge—this type of risk-taking is crucial in good design.

This living room exemplifies that concept by combining a bit of Americana with the flag, the layered rugs, and the tarnished silver vessels; a dash of Victorian with the couch; and a modern touch with the side table, the mini sawhorse table, and the paint-dipped ladder.

The layers and details in the room—such as the vintage hand-painted parrot figurine handed down from a great-grandmother, found books, and—of course—fresh flowers complete the serene setting.

CALLIOPE

PATCHWORK SOFA TABLE

A patchwork paper surface on furniture has been a signature look of mine for years. I wanted to take the technique in a new direction and give this piece a vintage, rustic look, so I intentionally chose Victorian and feminine floral papers for the patchwork.

I knew this sofa table would be mine the second I saw it. I mean, look at her! The oblong top, beautiful turned and scalloped legs, and scrollwork are perfection. I never pass up a sofa table from this era and with this body style—they have so much grace and beauty in their curves, and I find them irresistible. Most furniture is not made with this much thought and detail anymore, so it is meaningful to me to be able to bring new life to the details created by someone before me. The curves are beautiful in their original wood state; being painted completely transforms them into something magical. Since the piece was inherently feminine, I knew the patchwork top would fit perfectly.

My idea for the table was to go for a bit of a granny chic look. The challenge with this type of look is that most people see it as fitting for only a country, French, or shabby chic style. But I don't see it that way. I wanted to create a piece that is completely granny chic and place it in modern environments. I mixed a custom milk paint color in a pretty blue shade; then I chose five different papers with pretty little floral patterns. I went with lots of roses (roses just say "granny" to me) and chose five patterns to rotate within the design. Feel free to use however many patterns you'd like in your own work.

A collection of similar items—in this case, vintage clocks—makes for a compelling yet cohesive display.

IN THE LIVING ROOM

This sofa table works in its traditional role behind a sofa in a living room environment as a home to coasters, mail, sunglasses, keys, collections, plants, and artwork. For a table like this, try changing out the items every now and then to create a new style vignette and freshen up the room. The floral patchwork top, though a strong design element, does not take away from the rest of the room. The curves and floral pattern of the table paired with the modern straight-lined sofa make for an unexpected and compelling statement. When you enter this room, you notice not the back of the couch but rather the pretty table, which then draws your eye to the awesome vintage clock collection, oversized foliage arrangement, and colorful woven throw on the sofa back. Favorite colorful artwork is arrayed above the fireplace mantel. The floral armchair echoes the floral tabletop, giving a little nod to the granny chic look.

CALLIOPE / Patchwork Sofa Table

This patchwork table makes a lovely, unexpected desk that works especially well in a small living space such as a loft or apartment. Furniture pieces for smaller spaces generally need to have multiple uses and functions, so this table is a great fit for this space. It functions as a desk here, but in a pinch it could also work as a cozy dining table for two! Get used to the idea of moving furniture around and seeing how many ways you can use it in your space.

I find that when I sit at my desk to write, sketch, or create, I like to be comfortable and surrounded by things that inspire me and are meaningful. Here, found seashells sit in a wire basket nearby, special books and artwork surround the setting, and feathers from a friend's farm are cleverly taped to the wall. An industrial table lamp juxtaposes the traditional floral patterns of the tabletop and the decorative details drawn from nature. The mustard vintage chair provides a comfortable seat to work from and a fabulous pop of color. I absolutely love how this sweet little table looks placed in front of a giant loft window and exposed brick walls. The light from the window floods onto the desk, and the ample sill works like a shelf for extra storage and display.

Natural elements— such as feathers, shells, plants, and rocks—bring a sense of groundedness to a space and help spark inspiration.

CALLIOPE / Patchwork Sofa Table

A simple way to create depth is to
layer, layer, layer. The artwork, paper
patchwork, textiles, and florals in
this room create a cozy visual feast.   35

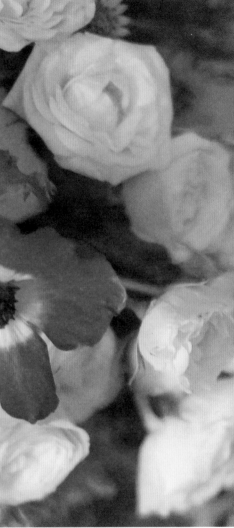

IN THE DEN

The masculine pine paneling on the walls of this den seem like they would contradict a pretty floral tabletop. But I see it differently. The knotty warmth of the walls reminds me of being in the woods where sunshine pierces through the trees' leafy canopy. The flowered table then becomes almost like a carpet of flowers on the forest floor, and the result is inviting and magical. In rooms where there is not a lot of built-in storage or shelving, a table like this provides space for displaying collections on top and an additional level of storage underneath.

The vintage Eames lounge chair is almost an act of rebellion in this space. How can something so modern mix with something so soft and traditional? It turns out that the most beautiful settings usually come from unexpected pairings. The patterned wool rug brings in color and anchors the room, while the heirloom bamboo and wooden rocking horse hints at the presence of little ones. The artwork created by a talented close friend, the vintage couch from a mid-century resale shop, and the soft throws—all of these details are either found or passed down and come together to create an inviting, cozy space that says "home."

BANKSY

This super clean and modern desk was part of the same bedroom set as the Map-Papered Dresser (page 117), Gold-Flecked Side Table (page 21), and City Skyline Dresser (page 61). As a furniture designer and collector, I am always excited when I can purchase several amazing pieces at once. I love the fact that each one of these pieces turned into a stunning and unique piece on its own instead of remaining part of a matching set.

Graffiti represents revolution, rebellion, and freedom. The original design of this desk seems conservative and traditional due to its straight lines, dark glass top, and straitlaced original hardware, so it was the perfect candidate for a graffiti design. I chose feminine colors for the paint—jewel tones of pink, yellow, green, gold, and purple—to go a little softer than expected and achieve something like "graffiti glam." My vision was to create layers and layers of color through patterns and symbols. I enlisted the help of my friends Angie and Lily, and we spent a few days layering color and design elements such as numbers, arrows, letters, eyes, speckles, and geometric patterns. It was so much fun to make, and in the end we had a totally original masterpiece! One of the best things about any graffiti project is that if you don't like a certain aspect, you can just paint over it.

I chose to keep the original hardware on this piece, since it is so natural and unassuming. To make it fit a little better with the design, I spray-painted the hardware peacock blue. I also switched out the original black glass top for a piece of clear glass cut to the exact same measurements. The black glass felt dated, plus the clear glass allows you to see and admire all of the beautiful graffiti work.

Even though the design of this desk is busy, it's actually quite versatile in both style and function.

I always prefer off-kilter groupings of
bottles and glassware over perfect and
precise displays.

IN THE DINING ROOM

The size of this desk and the vibrant colors make it a great fit for a modern loft environment as a sideboard server and bar. Since storage is at a premium in a small space such as a loft, this desk becomes multifunctional, with drawers for storing linens, silverware, glassware, and bottle openers. It's an eye-catching place to display all of your pretty barware and drinks for a cocktail or dinner party. A pair of white side chairs with graphic black-and-white pillows encourages guests to sit and stay for a spell, while the giant elk skull wearing a handmade feather headpiece seems to say "Fun happens here!" You might think a black-and-white cowhide rug would be too much pattern with the graffiti desk, but they actually balance each other perfectly. Black-and-white accessories are always easy to mix and match.

BANKSY / Graffiti Desk

This entire display
highlights collected
and gathered favorites,
reflecting the person-
ality of the owner and
popping cheerfully
against that white
wall.

IN THE HOME OFFICE

Even with the graffiti treatment, this piece works beautifully for its original function as a desk. In this home office, I added some natural oak shelves above to provide more storage and space to display collections and creative inspiration. Keeping the shelves in their natural wood state adds a clean modern neutral next to the colorful desk. I love for my workspace to be clean, bright, and inspiring, and these shelves help keep everything organized. I always have tons of paper around, so I placed a nice large basket beside the desk for stashing pretty papers—it also adds visual interest to the room. The vintage floor lamp and metal chair add a cool touch to the very warm desk colors. Here again you see the pleasing combination of wood, glass, and metal. There are enough drawers to store office supplies, and the surface is large enough for a computer. With this desk, sitting down to work each day becomes much more fun.

Metallic accessories add contrast and help reflect the colors of this paint finish.

43

IN THE BEDROOM

A desk can easily double as a vanity or dressing station. Hang a colorful mirror above the piece, display all of your favorite perfume and jewelry on the top, and stash away your makeup, brushes, and beauty necessities in the numerous drawers. Top off the look with a sweet little stool or chair. I particularly love how the hairpin legs and shibori-dyed fabric of this stool harmonize with the graffiti patterns on the desk. Don't be afraid to mix and match patterns—go for a "so wrong it's right" effect as much as you can. The bright green oak mirror adds a nice pop of color that unifies the look, and the scrolled detail on the mirror frame brings a beautiful softness. I like to decorate the mirror on my vanity with favorite photos and quotes because it gives me a nice little lift at the beginning of each day.

SPURGEON

TECHNIQUES

- - - - - - -

APPLYING MILK PAINT
(page 160)

My dad brought this pew back for me after visiting a historical church in upstate New York. I had been looking for a bench for my eat-in kitchen, and this pew was perfect. I fell in love with the scrolled back and sides, and when I spied a little metal number thirty-three on the side, I admit I actually did a skip and a jump. I love numbers as design elements, so the perfect pew plus numbers made this the score of the year.

Church pews—often seen as stiff or stuffy—actually make for unexpectedly versatile and comfortable seating. Once you add a nice soft cushion, the pew becomes a lovely bench that invites friends and family to sit down and enjoy the moment.

I created the design plan for this piece with my own house in mind. My cabinets are a distressed cream with a tobacco glaze, and my table is a natural wood farm table, so I wanted to create something warm and rustic. I chose a cool gray for the pew and a plaid flannel for the seat pad. The pew came with the original red velvet seat pad, which we used as a template to recover it with the flannel. I love wearing flannel shirts in the autumn and winter, and I wanted this seat to feel as cozy and soft as a favorite flannel shirt.

For the wooden surface of the pew, I created a custom milk paint color by mixing black and white milk paints until I achieved the perfect shade of gray. The grays and blues in this particular flannel work perfectly with the painted color of the wood.

IN THE KITCHEN

This church pew makes a beautiful bench for dining when paired with a modern farm table. The combination of an antique traditional pew with a contemporary table brings interest to the room. A simple wooden bench provides additional seating but does not compete with the other design elements in the room. The giant Stendig calendar keeps things graphic and modern, while the sweet original tulip light is a nod to the past. A set of vintage kilim and patchwork pillows provide a soft place to land on the bench seat. To emphasize the home-spun feeling, I set the table with hand-carved wooden plates and hand-pinched ceramic bowls. Fresh flowers bring color, life, and beauty to any table setting. I try to keep a bunch of flowers on my table at all times.

Aging vintage textiles, as seen on these throw pillows, add textural appeal and get a whole new life in this setting.

Mixing found items within
a color palette brings
intentionality to a vignette.

ON THE PORCH

I have always dreamed of having a big wrap-around porch. If I ever do get the old farmhouse of my fantasies, this is the type of setting I will create. When I first saw the church pew, I didn't immediately envision it for an outdoor setting. But there is just something special about a comfortable porch setting. The length of the pew fills the length of the porch and makes it look full and inviting. A soft, cheerful rug underfoot adds color while at the same time making the environment feel more like an additional room. Comfortable throw pillows are a must, and the oversize outlaw portraits on them add a touch of quirkiness to the scene. A vintage chicken crate coffee table holds extra books, magazines, and fresh floral clippings and adds warmth and a sense of history to the space. A little painted wooden stool doubles as a footrest or a tiny side table. This spot is ideal for morning tea and reading.

Woven rugs don't have to be on the floor to bring visual interest to a space—try rolling up your favorites and displaying in a crate or basket.

IN THE ENTRY

A pew in a foyer or entryway provides an easy and attractive place for family members and visitors to sit down and tie shoes or take off muddy boots. Place a few wall hooks above the bench to hang bags, hats, coats, and scarves. This ceramic hand wall hook is quirky and fun, adding a surprising little wink to the space. Use the space underneath the pew for anything you need to grab in a jiffy as you make your way out the door. You could keep a bin or urn for umbrellas nearby. The colorful wool rug pairs beautifully with a large mixed-media original art piece. To change up the look of the pew, I replaced the flannel seating pad with indigo dyed pillows for a more utilitarian design that fits this entry space.

BENRADINE

TECHNIQUES

- - - - - - -

OMBRÉ LETTERING
(page 162)

DISTRESSING
(page 151)

I was drawn to this coffee table for its clean lines and smooth, seamless surface. It translated into a beautiful blank canvas on which I quickly envisioned a fun grouping of words. I almost took off the sweet little metal floral accent but then decided against it, as it softens the lines of the piece with a special detail.

I love lots of different shades of blue together, so my idea was to create a blue ombré quote that would peek out through a white surface paint. For the quote, I wanted something inspirational and positive—something that would inspire me every day when I walked past the table. I've always loved the Mary Oliver line "As though I had wings"; it makes me daydream about flying to faraway places and exploring the world. I chose the white and blue combination because it is uplifting and gives the piece a versatility that can be incorporated into multiple settings. The finished piece really makes a statement—literally!

For the den, I decided to turn the coffee table into a bookshelf by simply placing it against a wall. This type of setup works great in both large and small rooms and provides a cozy nook for reading and relaxing. I styled it with favorite old photos attached to the wall with washi tape, a vintage brass lamp for light, some mismatched pillows to lounge on, a soft and colorful rug on the floor, and a candle for some extra glow in the evenings while relaxing or gathering with friends. The overall effect is warm and cozy—I can see this quickly becoming a favorite spot in any house.

Frames aren't always necessary for a photo display—tape favorite family photos to the wall and change them around as you please.

This oversized ottoman provides a place to prop tired feet, comes in handy as extra seating, and also makes a design statement.

IN THE LIVING ROOM

This table works wonderfully in its traditional function in this gorgeous and bright living room setting. I placed it in front of the white slip-covered couch and minimally styled the setting with fresh flowers and brass animals. A coffee table is the perfect place to display favorite objects, books, and knickknacks that tell your story. This living room is busy and eclectic, with bookshelves full of artwork, a comfortable rocking chair, a geometric otto-man, large potted fig plants, and found gems, so it works best to keep the surface of the coffee table fairly bare. This way, everyone can see the inspiring quote on the surface—and besides, you always need a spot to prop your feet up after a long day.

BENRADINE / Quote Coffee Table

I love these little daisies
with this pink floral bedspread.
Sometimes it's okay to go girly!

59

IN THE BEDROOM

This coffee table works beautifully
at the foot of the bed, where it not
only looks good but also creates a bit
of extra surface and storage space.
It's a great place for extra blankets,
throw pillows, a potted plant, and
vintage candlesticks, and you can
stash shoes and pillows underneath.
The straight lines of the table look
lovely in this environment, paired
with layered bright pink linens on a
vintage iron bed. The sweetness of
the setting is balanced out by the
graphic look of the quote, yet the
whites and blues of the table mix
seamlessly with the other colors in
the room. The wooden candlesticks
from Bali and pillows from Peru lend
a winning harmony to the space.

BLEECKER

CITY SKYLINE DRESSER

I love visiting and exploring big cities. Adding a city skyline to a piece is an idea I've had for a while. It's a tribute to one of my favorite hobbies—traveling—and makes for a unique and modern design. I knew I didn't want to paint just the front of a piece; I had to carry the design all the way around to give it real presence. When I saw this dresser, I knew it was an ideal canvas for the wraparound design because the drawers and sides are nice and flat. Rather than replicating a specific city, I decided on an abstract skyline to give it a modern, graphic feel that could be interpreted as a city or simply a geometric design. The creams and pinks contradict and soften the image of big looming buildings. It was fun to use basic materials and tools like tape, rulers, and stencils to create something totally fresh and different.

My great-grandmother's dough bowl gains
a new use on top of this dresser as an
eye-catching display and fruit bowl.

A fresh garland casually draped down
the table brings the outdoors in and
is an instant centerpiece.

IN THE DINING ROOM

This dresser is an unexpectedly appropriate addition to a dining room.
We chose a smaller dining room where a larger piece like a hutch or china
cabinet would crowd or overwhelm the space. The City Skyline Dresser
serves the same function while commanding less space. The graphic
pattern brings color and character, allowing the piece to become the
design focal point of the room. It also provides much-needed storage
space for linens, extra serving pieces, barware, and seasonal necessities.
The space on top can be kept simple and clean with a wooden bowl full
of lemons, or you can create a style vignette with artwork, dishware,
glassware, and other collections. The pinks of the city skyline echo the
shades found in the colorful rug. The result: a room that is urban yet
cozy and inviting.

Use your imagination
when displaying
everyday objects—
your jewelry can
become instant art!

Hanging favorite drawings
from your sketchbook highlights moments of inspiration
and provides affordable art
for your home.

IN THE BEDROOM

The painted white brick walls in this bedroom are modern and clean and perfectly complement the lines of this dresser. The softness of the flokati rug and round mid-century mirror provide a welcome contrast to all the straight angles in the dresser design. The mustard and brown pillows add another mid-century touch and bring out the pink in the dresser, adding a fun hit of color to the space. The antlers add unexpected personality, and the glass bottles double as jewelry holders, bringing both style and function to the dresser top.

Bright and exuberant florals add a
burst of personality to the layers of
art in this room.

67

IN THE DEN

Adding some shelving above for artwork,
photographs, and knickknacks transforms this
dresser into a stylish and functional entertainment center. Store records and remotes
in the drawers for a clean look, free of cords
and appliances. With a simple TV or stereo
on top, the focus becomes the beauty of
the piece rather than the electronics. A few
magnolia leaves sprayed with gold paint and
taped to the wall add a really pretty design
element from nature, further beautifying the
space. The overall effect is one of calm and
coziness, and the dresser quickly blends in as
a functional part of the room.

CHARISTEO

WEATHERED DINING TABLE

TECHNIQUES
- - - - - - - -

WEATHERING WITH PAINT
(page 166)

This lovely dining table was a side-of-the road find. I absolutely love the detailed pedestal legs and the carved apron around the base of the top. It was obvious that this table had been outside in the elements for quite some time—the wood was sun bleached, rough, and naturally weathered. A heavily sanded and distressed finish was the perfect choice. You can use this technique on any wood piece—it doesn't need to be naturally worn—but I loved adding to the existing character, and I knew the raised and porous grain in the wood would suck up the paint for the look I was after. I wanted this table to work in many different settings, and I designed the piece with that in mind.

Traditional ideas of where to
place furniture can keep you
from fully utilizing space in
your home. Break the rules!

IN THE LIVING ROOM

Dining tables actually make terrific, spacious desks, and the size of this particular table works beautifully as a desk in this gorgeous living room. The fantastic natural light streaming through the front door just bathes this whole setting in beauty. Who wouldn't want to sit here and work away? I believe desks should always be placed in a clean, inspiring space where you feel comfortable and motivated to work. This setting absolutely fits that description. The giant turquoise and yellow finch painting provides an inspiring focal point—I can imagine just staring into the magical land of the finches when in need of a little inspiration. The red geometric design of the director's chair brings color and clean functional lines to the setting. The unique shape of the mid-century lamp provides a sleek contrast to the hominess of the vintage globe, collection of favorite sketchbooks and pencils, and tiny ceramic vessels. This desk landscape is full of warm, thoughtful details—one advantage of using a larger table for a workspace. The comfy turquoise armchair welcomes visitors or clients to take a seat and is a great spot to curl up for a break to invite creative inspiration.

IN AN EAT-IN KITCHEN

This table is right at home in this kitchen. The natural wood grain of the table pairs seamlessly with the wood floor and bent plywood chairs. The bits of the original painted finish that remain on the tabletop add hints of color and fun little details. The large window lets in gorgeous natural light and sheds warmth on the giant fiddle leaf fig towering in the corner. Pretty artwork in rich warm golden tones complements the earthiness of the space, and a black mid-century pendant lamp lends some weight and grounds the look. Having a good-sized table in the kitchen area provides extra serving and sitting space for large parties, and it can also be a cozy environment for small family meals.

CHARISTEO / Weathered Dining Table

I chose not to use a tablecloth because I wanted the beauty of the table to show and become part of the experience, but beautiful linens can be used in this type of setting as well.

FURNITURE MAKES THE ROOM

OUTSIDE

You don't have to rely on patio furniture when hosting an outdoor dinner party. The smaller size of this table makes it fairly easy to move from room to room, and when placed outside it provides a lovely setting for a summer meal. The wood grain blends perfectly into the natural surroundings. I placed an outdoor rug under the table because it creates a roomlike environment and adds warmth and softness underfoot. I also pulled out my collection of vintage French bistro chairs. The pillows can provide extra comfort, and the table setting, with candles and wooden bowls full of fruit, cheese, and bread, welcomes guests to sit down and relax. I kept this setting really clean and simple with the wooden dishes, but any type of ceramic dish or china can be used for outdoor dining. Next time you want to dine al fresco, think about letting your dining table moonlight as an outdoor table for the night.

THE FOUR & TWENTY BLACKBIRDS PIE BOOK

FURNITURE MAKEOVERS

apartment therapy

BOUCHE

BOOKCASE DRESSER

This dresser had seen better days when I found it. The bottom drawer was damaged and could not bear weight without major structural repairs. I didn't notice the damage initially when I purchased the piece, since it was on the bottom and hidden from sight (yes, this happens even to me!). But I was smitten with the piece's curvy and voluptuous base and determined to find a new use for her. She was actually a great candidate for converting a dresser into a bookcase, since the drawers must be removed for that anyway. It took a bit of work to remove the center section and add sturdier plywood shelving, but it was worth it to get this whimsical bookcase in the end. I chose to paint the outside of this piece pumpkin and the inside a really pale pink—multiple colors bring an element of surprise. Plus, orange and pink is one of my favorite color combinations. The piece has a bit of a French flair, so I chose milk paint for the outside to give it that layered, textured, country look. It's hard to find unique bookshelves these days. Creating one from an interesting dresser solves that problem and results in a budget-friendly piece with a story and a purpose.

IN THE BEDROOM

At first glance, you may not visualize this shelf working in a modern bedroom setting, given its pumpkin orange and pink palette and natural curves. But it works beautifully in this bedroom when paired with geometric bedding, a kilim rug, shag pillows, and a sweet little golden stool. The dark paint on the walls allows the colors to pop, while white velvet drapes (yes, velvet!) bring a luxurious feel and both elevate and balance the room. Filled to the brim with soft-colored vintage books, shed antlers, and white ceramic figurines, the shelf looks right at home here. The top provides the perfect place to rest a treasured piece of art, a plant, and a modern lamp with clean lines. It may be unexpected, but I love the way the piece works in this room.

This bookshelf display is perfection—thoughtful, eclectic, and functional.

BOUCHE / Bookcase Dresser

Don't be afraid to layer bold black-and-white over pretty colorful patterns.

IN THE DEN

Set against a backdrop of whimsical wallpaper with big bears riding little bikes, the bookcase takes on a whole new look in this den. The colors in the wall pattern bring out the colors in the piece, creating a relaxed, friendly vibe. The den is where families tend to spend the most time together—at least that's the way it is in our house—so the shelves are full of things collected and loved. A hand-drawn charcoal cicada adds a bit of black and white and works with the black-and-white striped chair and the black-and-white graphics on the door. The found wool rug with shades of green, peach, pink, blue, and black ties the look together, making this an eclectic and cozy family space.

IN THE KITCHEN

Placed right next to the counter in the kitchen and filled with stacks of colorful dishes and dishcloths, this bookcase brings visual interest to the room while providing extra cabinet space. Open shelving in a kitchen is functional and creates a casual, relaxed atmosphere. The shelf is a beautiful place to display colorful vintage dishware and pots and pans. There is also plenty of room for tea towels, plants, and cookbooks. The look is vibrant and modern, with a touch of down-home country, making the kitchen feel nurturing, warm, and alive. I also love the collection of little plants on top!

Tea towels don't have to be hung to be displayed. A stack of favorite patterned tea towels brings color and texture to this collection.

PIEDRA

SCALLOPED SIDEBOARD

TECHNIQUES
- - - - - - - -

SCALLOPED DIP-DYEING
(page 170)

WOOD FILLING
(page 150)

LINING DRAWERS
(page 152)

I never pass up sideboards like this—they are absolutely my favorite type of furniture to paint. Large, typically ornate, and always full of character in their design, sideboards make it easy to come up with a fresh, modern design plan. For this piece I wanted to create a line of demarcation with the paint, but I decided I didn't want to do a straight line. I wanted it to be playful and fun, with a nod to the curve of the legs and skirt. I chose a scalloped line for the bottom of the piece to draw attention to the pretty base, especially the curved legs. A scalloped line at the top would not have been as soft and appealing. When choosing where to place a line of demarcation, I always gravitate toward a less dramatic, more asymmetrical effect. It is more interesting when a line doesn't divide a piece perfectly down (or across) the middle. Placement can be everything when pulling off this type of design.

This sideboard is a workhorse! The top has ample space, the inside is roomy and provides tons of storage, and like most sideboards it has drawers for storage as well. You may think that the bright jade green color limits the versatility of this piece, but as you will soon see, jade becomes a neutral in the right settings. Soon you'll want to paint multiple pieces in your home this very color. Also, the little bit of wood left exposed at the base adds a rich warmth that makes it even more versatile.

IN THE KITCHEN

Check out how fabulous this piece looks in this bright and airy farmhouse kitchen. It's a clear example of eclectic yet stylish living. First of all, the round painting of the playful fox jumping over the chicken adds a hit of rich color that complements the deep jade tones of the sideboard. Antique crocks full of kitchen utensils and vintage silver assembled next to the morning's gathering of eggs and a collection of favorite cookbooks create a peaceful and laid-back setting. The jade color, scalloped detail, and golden knobs of the sideboard blend beautifully with the eclectic nature of the room while at the same time providing a place for the mixer, cookbooks, and extra table linens.

The bright white kitchen is an ideal backdrop for a pop of color.

This is the perfect example of giving a statement piece a real function.

FURNITURE MAKES THE ROOM

IN THE DINING ROOM

This jade green simply glows against a black wall. The moodiness and drama created by the dark walls, the vibrant hues of the painting, and the mid-century globe light pair with the sideboard for a modern yet romantic effect. Again, the sweetness of the scalloped edge of the sideboard is balanced out by the heaviness of the color in the room. The warm wood of the antique table and chairs as well as the indigo rug add to the richness and gem-toned color palette.

IN THE **NURSERY**

At first this piece may seem too sophisticated for a baby's room, but, trust me, it can fit right in as a changing table. In this nursery, hues of sage, mint, and jade come together for a sweet and calming effect. I love the collection of artwork above the changing table—it is colorful and whimsical and reflects a love of all things vintage and handmade. The utilitarian red light fixture hanging from the wall brings a modern touch. The ample surface space of this sideboard is perfect for use as a changing table, and the storage space below hides away diapers, blankets, and baby essentials. This is a piece that can truly grow with your child—or end up in another room of your house one day. When working with pieces for a nursery, I always suggest thinking "big picture" and creating a piece that can be moved around and changed over time as the seasons of life change.

Special details like a tiny paper garland, vintage figurines, geometric mobile, and stuffed elephant sweeten this gender-neutral nursery.

91

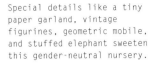

PIEDRA / Scalloped Sideboard

SHIKOBA

FEATHER DECAL ARMOIRE

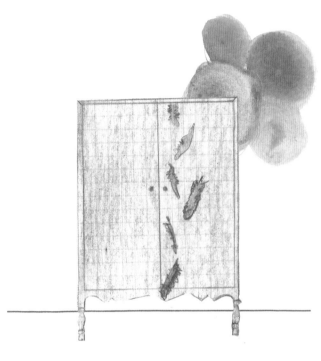

TECHNIQUES
- - - - - - - -

APPLYING DECALS
(page 172)

WOOD FILLING
(page 150)

APPLYING WALLPAPER TO
DRAWER FRONTS (page 181)

Small armoires like this are getting harder to find, so when a friend called and said that he wanted to get rid of this piece, I jumped at the chance to purchase it. I am a lover of detail in furniture, and this miniature armoire is full of character, with the inside drawers, long turned legs, and carved elements. As we rethink our homes to make them more livable and sustainable, pieces like this little armoire become increasingly more desirable because they are durable yet multifunctional. This armoire can go beside a bed and act as a side table and dresser all in one, provide beauty and storage in a craft room, or nestle into a corner of the kitchen to hold supplies.

Navy is a timeless classic, and gold is beautiful with everything, but especially when paired with dark colors like navy and black. I am always trying to think of how I can completely redesign a piece and push the design juxtaposition. This armoire felt ornately feminine, so I chose a bold navy to offset that. Applying gold feather wall decals was a fast and easy way to get high design for low commitment and cost. The gold feathers look modern on their own, but when they are applied in an artistic falling pattern, the entire piece becomes ethereal. If you tire of the feathers, you can remove them and still have a beautiful navy armoire. I wallpapered the three drawer fronts on the inside of the piece because details matter so much. Now when you open the doors to this piece, you're greeted with surprise details.

The glimmer of the gold foil
reflects light and gives
movement to the feathers.

IN THE LIVING ROOM

In this room, a pair of tall modern wingbacks flanks the armoire, commanding full attention. Their clean lines, color, and weight complement
the curves and moodiness of the armoire. This piece functions as a display
cabinet for a treasured collection of handmade pottery from artists all
over the country. The drawers store art books, magazine articles, maps
of art districts, and inspiration files. The rustic pottery collection brings
depth, texture, and warmth to the setting. Each pottery piece has a story,
including where it was purchased or found, how it was made, and the
maker who formed it. This type of collection needs to be on display and
stands out beautifully from the dark color of this piece. The rich tones of
brown and cream in the cowhide rug and the little organic wooden side
tables bring natural, grounding elements to the space without over-
whelming it or crowding it in the least.

The modern, layered, uncluttered
aesthetic of this studio is calming
and inspiring.

IN AN ART STUDIO

This unique armoire is totally in its element in an art studio, placed against the backdrop of a gorgeous landscape painting. The whimsical design of the piece makes it a great choice for anyone looking for a pretty alternative to conventional storage options in a studio. The piece itself is a work of art, so it brings an element of creative inspiration to the room while also providing a place to store paints, brushes, canvases, and supplies. The internal drawers and cubbies house all sorts of materials, allowing for an organization system that is neatly tucked out of view so the focus can be on creating. The motion of the feathers speaks to the motion of paints and energy in this type of artistic space.

SHIKOBA / Feather Decal Armoire

Navy is a strong
color and grounds
this eclectic
space.

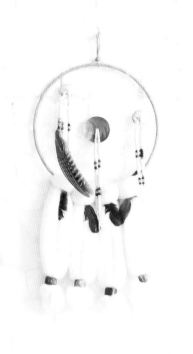

IN THE BEDROOM

In its more expected bedroom setting, this armoire takes on the roles of both a side table and a chest of drawers. The rich wood and simple curves of the bed blend nicely with the many curves and artistic elements of the armoire. The hammered bronze plant stand brightens up the corner and plays off of the gold feather pattern on the door front. The room is spare, clean, and modern, and the armoire contributes by providing concealed storage for extra blankets. It also functions as a dresser, with drawers for clothing and a flat surface to display treasured artwork and vintage finds. I just love the long soft wool runner with its black, cream, rust, and turquoise colors. This rug softens the space with its texture and adds a nice pattern contrast with the stripes on the papered drawer fronts and the golden feathers of the armoire.

FERATORIA

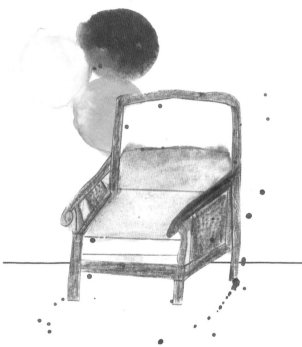

TECHNIQUES

- - - - - - - -

STRIPPING PAINT
(page 174)

I purchased this chair from an estate sale, and it was definitely sad in its "before" state. Many coats of paint had been layered onto the wood, and the final layer was a glossy black that just was not appealing. The upholstery job was a serious case of DIY gone wrong, and the fabric was long past its prime. I immediately wanted to take this chair from being painted to unpainted—to expose and refresh the natural wood. I also wanted to use a custom fabric for the seat. I commissioned my friend Angie to dye the fabric for me, and she created this beautiful shibori pattern. Once the chair was fully stripped and the new fabric was ready, I took it to my upholsterer to finish the job.

When the re-created chair was finished, with the new rustic combination of natural wood and fresh dyed linen, I had to step back and let my eyes adjust. Can you even believe this is the same chair? I can't. It's natural yet modern, a solid piece that works in a myriad of settings.

Linen napkins with
a hand-painted arrow
design complement the
gold tones on the
tabletop and complete
the place setting.

AT THE TABLE

Placed at the head of the table, this chair is an inviting spot that everyone will be fighting over. Don't be afraid to mix and match chair styles around a table—it's charming and inviting, an instant icebreaker. To pull off the mismatched look, try to stay within a single color palette, whether it be all different kinds of wood or painted shades, and make sure the table and chairs complement each other in size and structure. For instance, you would not want to pair a huge, solid pub table with little spindly chairs.

Taking its place at an antique oak pedestal table, this indigo chair commands attention. The table is set with cream china and a simple gray linen runner, but the real fun comes from the collection of brass animals in the center, each one lovingly hand picked.

FERATORIA / Stripped Indigo Chair

IN THE FOYER

The walls of this foyer are completely covered with flower and moth designs, hand drawn with a gold Sharpie directly onto the wall. The effect is absolutely spellbinding. These loopy lines provide a subtle yet visually interesting backdrop for the indigo chair. I love how the blue pops against the mustard and gold tones, almost like a jewel in the room. The oversized potted fig and bright red rug make for a cozy little seating corner or reading nook.

Hand-drawn walls
are one-of-a-
kind and a great
conversation
starter.

IN THE DEN

This soft, bright, and airy den works well for many reasons. For one, we have the perfect balance of wood, metal, and glass. The industrial coffee table sits in perfect juxtaposition with the gleaming vintage brass lamp, warm round woven rug, and natural wood of the chair. There is no tension between the modern couch and the chair because even though the chair is not modern in form, it is clearly modern in design. The pink tones in the large piece of artwork by a local artist subtly echo the neutral couch. Fresh flowers and houseplants complete the look and welcome you into the room.

The light, space, and neutral tones in this room have a truly calming effect.

EVERLY

CHALKBOARD BED

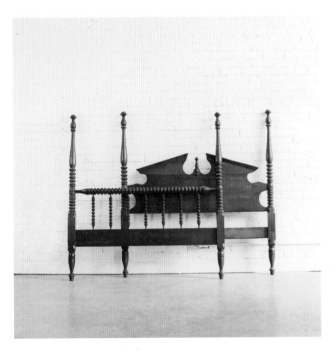

TECHNIQUES
- - - - - - -

APPLYING CHALKBOARD PAINT
(page 176)

This bed is traditional in its shape and form: it is a federal-style bed with a mahogany finish, and the curves and arches are meant to be formal and fancy. The way my mind works, though, is to take this traditional bed and do something completely opposite, to make it fresh, fun, and useful in multiple locations. I think I am sometimes drawn to these traditional pieces because so many people have them and hate them! I love showing people how to see things completely differently. How opposite can you get from stiff and federal? Well, how about letting kids and adults write on the bed? Isn't that fun? All you need is a few coats of paint and some chalk.

I wanted to keep the bed playful yet tasteful, so I used chalkboard paint only inside the inset of the headboard, where there were nice starting and stopping lines. I kept the rest of the bed a pretty slate blue. Using a darker color keeps the bed a little bit more rich and still polished, but in a casual way.

IN A
KID'S BEDROOM

The chalkboard aspect of this bed's design evokes playfulness and whimsy that make it a great candidate for a young child's room. Most children I know love to doodle and draw. Drawing on furniture is usually a big no-no, but with this piece, it is totally allowed. What joy for your children and their friends! The fun patterned wallpaper decorated with children's artwork adds to the environment of creativity. The bright golden yellow bedding and pink dinosaur pillow add brightness to the room but pair nicely with the calming gray blue of the bed. Because the bedding and accessories are so colorful, a natural jute rug works to bring balance to the room. Design is all about give and take—a little bright here, a little neutral there. A small wood nightstand holds books and a lamp for bedtime reading. This room provides a relaxed and comfortable environment that encourages daydreaming and play.

The cracked and peeling walls in
this historic home bring depth and
magic. Perfection is never the goal!

FURNITURE MAKES THE ROOM

IN A GROWN-UP BEDROOM

Your bedroom should be comfortable—the place where you feel you can let your hair down and be yourself. This bedroom's high ceiling, large windows, and bare, chipped plaster walls let the bed take center stage. It has all of the bedroom necessities, but none of the excess that so often accompanies formal furniture styles, and that's what makes it so inviting. The colorful wool kilim rug, wood and iron side table, brass floor lamp, and oversized linen bedding all add up to an environment that feels authentic, lived in, and warm. I'm a firm believer that beds do not have to be made to perfection and smothered in pillows and shams to look nice. A couple of pillows are plenty to add color and comfort, and looser bedding is actually more appealing. The chalkboard headboard is a surprising detail: here you can write quotes, sparks of ideas, or little love notes to your sweetie.

The trick to this space is in
the layering of textures and
patterns, bringing hominess to
the vast outdoor surroundings.

ON A SCREENED PORCH

A bed on a screened porch? This may sound a little out there, but it actually isn't uncommon in the summertime in the South! For hot summer nights when the cicadas are singing, a porch bedroom is heavenly. This porch is high up in the trees right off the master bedroom; being here feels like you are in a magical tree house. Soft bedding, extra wool blankets, and a wool rug define the bedroom space and provide a warm spot for your feet as they touch the floor first thing in the morning. Bring out a bedside table and an ottoman or stool to hold all of your reading and treasures, just as you would in your indoor bedroom. All of the textures in the rugs, bedding, and blankets blend beautifully and make for a cozy outdoor setting while still being elegant.

to the light

BEAUFAIN

MAP-PAPERED DRESSER

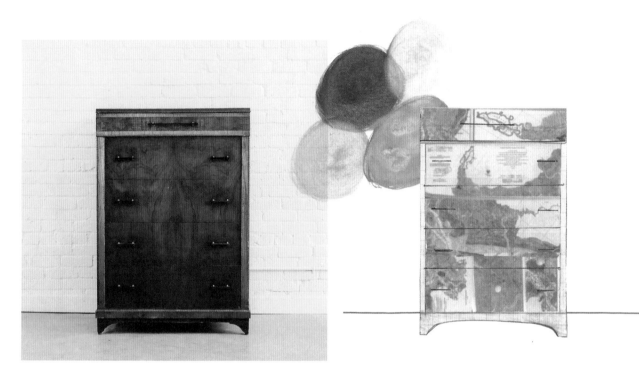

This tall mid-century dresser has flat-fronted drawers that are perfect for applying paper. The sides are also inset, which is another favorite detail of mine for papering because the trim of the furniture naturally frames the paper and provides a straight guideline for the application.

I loved this unique black-and-white map design and envisioned applying it all over a piece of furniture to create a graphic look that is not what you typically get with traditional maps. The result looks almost like marble. To make it extra personal, I chose coastal maps of South Carolina because that is home to me. The maps, featuring some of the very beaches that I love to visit in the summer with my family, were specifically created for me by a company called salt labs. The print-on-demand service Spoonflower (spoonflower.com) printed the paper—it is regular gift wrapping paper with no coating at all. I chose the nice, rich sepia and black tones for graphic interest. I kept the original hardware on this piece—it is black and gold and very handsome, and flows seamlessly with the look and color of the maps.

IN THE
LIVING ROOM

This bright living room is sparse and modern, with hints of deep, rich color. The black leather chairs and sofa are softened by the cheery yellow rug, brass floor lamp, and green fig plant. The blue, green, and gray in the watercolors are loose and fluid, adding an element of ease and beauty to the space. The chipped and peeling paint of the black and white lobster buoys add another layer of texture and bring an adventurous maritime feel that goes well with the large map motif. I think of this dresser as a centerpiece of functional art: it is visually striking and provides ample storage.

Air plants are the easiest
way to bring green to a space.
They require minimal water,
and look lovely hanging out on
a stack of books, atop a shelf,
or in your favorite vessel.

BEAUFAIN / Map-Papered Dresser

The colors and patterns of kilim rugs,
throws, and pillows have long been a
favorite of mine and work in nearly
every space.

121

IN THE MUDROOM

This farmhouse mudroom is a spacious stopping place for removing rubber boots and winter coats, setting down morning egg gatherings, and piling foraged herbs and flowers. You may not see a tall dresser in most mudrooms, but it actually makes perfect sense, given the ample storage it provides. Fill the drawers with gardening tools, gloves, cleaning supplies, scissors, floral wire, extra vases, and egg baskets. The room's seating works well with pillows on top, and there are bonus cubbies for stashing shoes and bags. Adding a few wall hooks for hanging bags and scarves completes the look of this functional yet stylish little room.

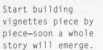

Start building
vignettes piece by
piece—soon a whole
story will emerge.

IN THE FOYER

This foyer is large enough to
house a tall dresser, and I love
the way it is styled with lots of
art and knickknacks—the instant
impression is one of hominess and
comfort. The map is nestled in a
little world of stories and adven-
tures: a hand-carved wooden bowl,
rocks collected on a family trip out
West, hand-forged iron pieces, and
treasured pottery and artwork. The
giant paned door lets in gorgeous
natural light that bathes the scene
of found and collected items. The
colorful rug balances out all of the
neutral tones and adds to the delicious spontaneity of the scene.

TWOMBLY

PAINTED SOFA

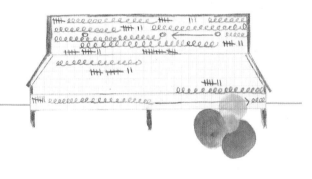

TECHNIQUES

- - - - - - -

PAINTING ON FABRIC
(page 182)

I had this couch sitting around the studio for years. It had great retro upholstery that I loved, but I thought it was time for a clean slate. I had always wanted to paint on fabric and create custom designs on upholstered pieces, and in this old sofa I saw the perfect opportunity to do something totally new. I enlisted the help of my sweet friend Annie Koelle, a talented local artist; we put our heads together and came up with a black-and-white painted pattern. I chose black because it is striking, commanding, and classic, and I knew it wouldn't detract from the piece or cause the finished product to turn out too trendy. Annie and I looked at several different patterns, including mountains, houses, and circles, but in the end we went with strikes, arrows, and loops because we liked the mixture of hard and soft lines and we felt the pattern had a balanced yet couture look. I had the sofa reupholstered in canvas drop cloth to literally provide a blank canvas for our vision.

I also decided to change the design of the upholstery. Instead of leaving three separate seat cushions, I chose to combine them all into one long seat. I like the clean modern lines and how this small change gave the piece a whole new look. I also chose to replace all of the small buttons and trim on the seat backs with just a few larger buttons. The big buttons still do their job in keeping the fabric taut, but they have a cleaner look. Don't be afraid to change things up!

Found architectural letters
are an easy way to add a
graphic touch. Paint them the
same color as the wall for
added sophistication.

IN THE BEDROOM

It's a luxury to have room for a sofa in the bedroom as an extra spot for relaxing or curling up with a book. In this setting, the warm, boldly patterned red rug highlights the more subtle pattern on the sofa in a "so wrong it's right" look. I loved the combination of patterns so much that I added more with the hand-dyed shibori pillows, multicolored vintage afghan, and side table with a papered drawer. The blue of the bed echoes the blue and white of the couch, providing a calming anchoring piece for the busyness of the rest of the setting. Taken all together, I find this room simply happy.

ON THE PORCH

Indoor/outdoor living is important to consider as we aim to use all the space in our homes. This big old mill house has a wonderfully wide covered front porch with aged wood floors and plenty of room for a comfortable couch and a couple of sitting chairs. The modern straight lines of this couch work beautifully with the worn wood porch floors and crackled white balusters. The jute rug is durable and stands up to the heavy foot traffic of a porch. The leather ottoman's rich color grounds the space and provides a spot for propping up your feet or setting a cup of tea. A round side table with a lamp provides light in the evenings for reading or chatting and a spot for potted plants, books, magazines, or drinks. The plushness of the sofa makes this feel more like a living space than hard wooden "outdoor" furniture would, and in effect actually increases the livable space of this home.

A rotating collection of pillows
in different colors, sizes, and
fabrics is versatile and allows
for spontaneity in design.

IN THE LIVING ROOM

This living room setting is perfectly glamorous and gleaming, which is why I love seeing this graphic black-and-white couch plopped right in the middle! The mirrored coffee table catches the light from all angles, creating a beautiful glow that plays off the tinsel and crepe paper garland strung across the fireplace. The gilded frames in the artwork gallery and the brass candlestick collection add to the metallic theme and bring their own share of warmth and glow to the room as well. The wooden floor glows softly, and hints of shine bounce off of the modern lamp in the corner and the throw pillows in silk marble prints, pink velvets, and gold sequins. The quirkiest piece in this room is the ceramic hoof end table. White, modern, and unexpected, it sits in witty juxtaposition with a rustic cowhide. This living room is a purposeful mix of mid-century, rustic, and Victorian styles, which is exactly why it works so well.

No fireplace? No problem. Set the mood by creating your own "fire" with chalkboard paint and chalk.

TETRIS

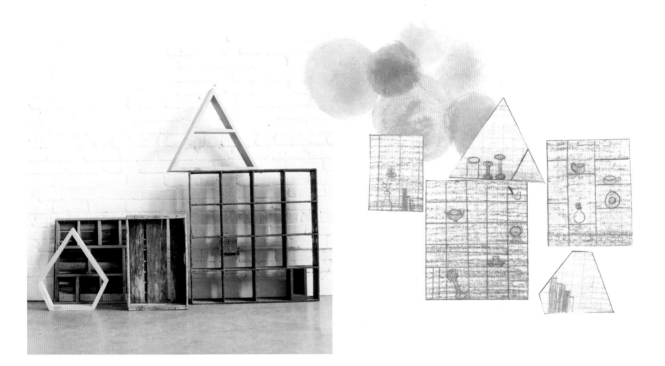

Using found crates, cubbies, and handmade wooden geometric pieces is a creative alternative to traditional shelving units, and an artful way to tell a style story. Mix and match the pieces and their contents to best suit their environment. I hand selected this grouping of light and dark woods. Apart from a light dusting and wipe-down, I used these exactly as I found them. Before I hung the shelves on the wall, I laid them out on the floor in different patterns and arrangements until I arrived at one that I liked; then I transferred them to the wall using a hammer, nails, and a level. There are endless ways to hang these pieces, and because of the different shapes and sizes, it's easy to transfer them from room to room and make them look completely new each time.

The first spot I thought of for these creative shelves was a boy's room—there's something about the geometric shapes and rugged style of the wood. In this bedroom—with its beautiful maple mid-century beds, matching nightstand, embroidered bedding, and vintage lamp—the wall installation of cubbies works as both décor and a display for favorite toys and objects of delight. All the little compartments make homes for Slinkies, cars, rock collections, a piggy bank, artwork, and books, with plenty of space for sliding in new treasures as they're found. I can just imagine feathers, shells, and more fun trinkets filling out the display over time. Plus, it's easy to swap out the contents as a boy grows and the room changes. This room is the perfect mixture of childlike and adult, which is my preferred approach for a kid's room—it says fun, but is still stylish and works well with the rest of the house.

The simplicity of this display looks effortless, yet was meticulously curated by color, texture, scale, and material.

TETRIS / Shelf Installation

Everyday kitchen items look
special when grouped and
displayed.

IN A KITCHEN

These little shelves work perfectly in a kitchen as a place to stash knick-knacks or spices. Open shelving in a kitchen is great for easy access and added decoration. Displayed in this kitchen are favorite found teacups, gold etched glasses, and other interesting glassware. It takes a bit of adding and editing to come up with a presentation that you like, but just keep moving things around, placing colors and textures together, until you are happy with the arrangement. The vintage breadbox, growlers from the local Community Tap, and apothecary bottles add some extra color to the scene. The randomness of this collection is what makes it so interesting—it tells the story unique to this family and home!

IN AN OFFICE

The configuration of boxes and crates hanging above a very modern desk works beautifully. I love how the gorgeous pattern of the wallpaper shows through the open-backed shelving, providing an interesting backdrop for a collection of quirky treasures such as an alligator head, vintage flashlights, an old pipe, wooden dumbbells, old family photographs, snuff scissors, and other relics. You can tell a lot about people by what they collect, and this display is sure to spark some interesting conversations with visitors and clients. A teakwood mid-century desk, colorful IKEA chair, vintage brass floor lamp, stack of encyclopedias, and jute rug all work together to complete this handsome space and bring balance to all of the details in the wall installation.

A fun wallpaper
pattern can bring
energy and action
to a space.

PART III

Toolbox

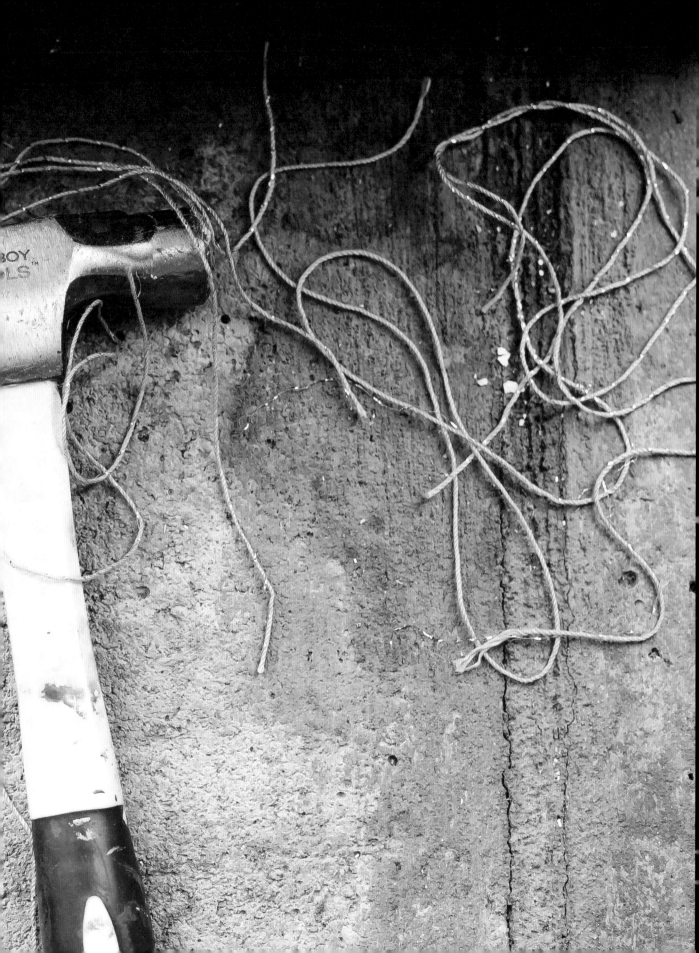

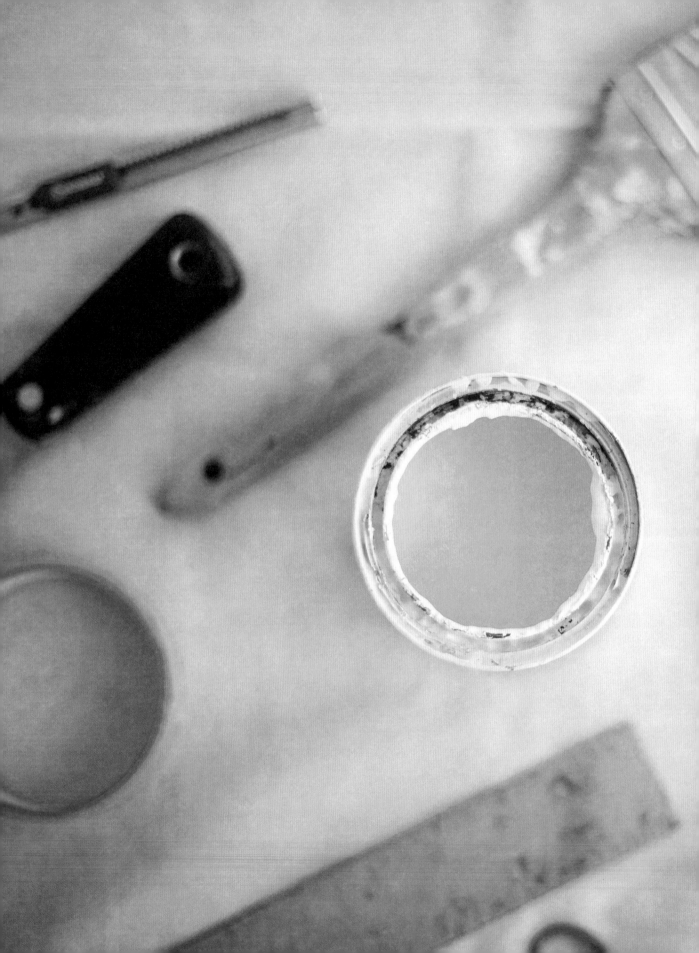

It is important to have the proper tools on hand in order to complete your projects in the best and most efficient way possible. It is terribly frustrating to get halfway through a project only to realize you are out of something essential or you do not have the proper tools to finish the job. Here I have listed all of the tools used to complete the projects outlined in this book. You may already have most of these tools on hand, but if not, you can find them at your local hardware or craft store. These are the tools that I use on a daily basis in my shop. It's a wise move to stock your toolbox and workbench with all of these before getting started.

PAINTING AND FINISHING

Canvas Drop Cloths

I like to keep things neat at the shop. Canvas drop cloths are perfect for keeping the floor underneath your furniture project nice and clean. I prefer canvas to paper or plastic or vinyl drop cloths because canvas can be washed and reused, plus you get the added bonus of really cool artwork when it is time to retire it. I have used my old painting cloths for wall art and to upholster furniture!

Citristrip

This natural, biodegradable stripping agent can knock out any stripping project and starts to work very quickly. I use Citristrip whenever I need to remove layers of paint, old varnish, or glue from a piece of furniture before applying a new painted finish.

Danish Oil

Danish oil is a wonderful product for protecting, sealing, and staining wood all in one step. I use the natural finish, since it does not add a whole lot of color. I use Danish oil mainly when I want to keep a natural wood surface but spruce it up a bit. The wonderful thing about Danish oil is that it penetrates the wood and works from the inside out. It hardens within the wood rather than on top of the wood. This makes it a great sealant and protector for any wood surface.

Foam Rollers

Foam rollers are used to create that ultrasmooth finish on furniture. They work great with latex and water-based finishes. However, rollers do not work well with milk paints, oils, or stains, since air can become trapped and leave a bubbled finish. On every piece of furniture that I paint, I use a foam roller for the large flat surfaces and a paintbrush for cutting in the corners. My motto with paint is "Less is more." The goal is to make the paint application become one with the wood, and foam rollers help achieve this outcome.

Furniture Wax

I use two different waxes in my furniture work. Fiddes is still my favorite brand for dark wax in the rugger brown color, but when I want a truly clear wax, Miss Mustard Seeds furniture wax is a great one to use. It is creamy, it has a lovely smell, and it melts into the paint surface beautifully. This is important in a wax finish. I prefer that wax be creamy and a bit on the wet side rather than dry and pastelike.

Gloves

When painting and staining, I keep three types of gloves on hand. I wear disposable plastic gloves when applying stains, to keep my hands clean. I use chemical-resistant gloves when working with stripping agents or other harsh chemicals. I also keep a nice pair of work gloves on hand for lifting or carrying wood furniture pieces that might cause splinters, doing rough sanding, and any other activity where my hands need an extra layer of protection.

Latex Paint

Latex is a water-based paint that provides great coverage; it is fast drying and widely available, and it can be cleaned up with soap and water. I work mainly with brands that have a high pigmentation and a creamy smooth consistency, like Benjamin Moore, Ralph Lauren, Behr, and Pratt & Lambert. I do not like to work with thick paints. I'm particular about the quality of paint that I use. It matters; I promise!

Measuring Cup

I use a 4-cup/960-ml see-through plastic measuring cup to measure out and mix all of my milk paint formulas.

Milk Paint

I have been using milk paint in my work since the early 2000s, and it is one of my favorite paints to work with! Milk paint gives a truly authentic finish that absolutely cannot be achieved with any other paint—a beautiful layered and peeled look that appears as if it took years and years to achieve. The finish tends to self-distress in a lovely way. Mixing milk paint is not complicated, as it is equal parts water and milk paint powder. It is an ecofriendly paint that is VOC free (free of volatile organic compounds) and leaves no odor when dry. Milk paint is available in twenty classic colors, but you can mix your own colors as well to create custom tints.

Mineral Spirits

I like to work with products that are as environmentally friendly as possible, and that can be challenging in the painting business! That is why I love this brand of mineral spirits by Klean-Strip. These mineral spirits are green: they have 65 percent less fumes than traditional spirits and 65 percent less VOC, and they are 65 percent more renewable. I use mineral spirits specifically for rinsing out my brushes when I have used oil-based products, and for

removing stripper residue when I am through stripping a piece of furniture.

Paintbrushes

I am very choosy about my paintbrushes, and I have used the same style and brand for the past fifteen years. You are free to use the paintbrush of your choice, but the Purdy 2½-in/6-cm angled sash brushes are my favorite for painting furniture. They allow me to get the smoothest finishes and very few paint lines. You will need several different kinds of brushes for furniture painting: small flat brushes for those hard-to-reach places, tiny brushes for detail work, sash brushes for the larger surfaces, and wax brushes for applying wax finishes.

Paint Trays

When using a foam roller, or any roller system for that matter, you will need a paint tray to hold your paint. Paint trays allow you to control the amount of paint on your roller and ensure that the roller is evenly coated for application. I buy plastic paint trays at my local hardware store because they are supereasy to rinse out and keep relatively clean. Since I mostly use latex and water-based products in my work, a soap-and-water cleanup is all that is needed. If you do not like to clean out your trays after painting, you can buy ecofriendly disposable and biodegradable liners for your paint trays that make cleanup even faster and easier!

Polyurethane

Polyurethane is a very durable synthetic resin finish with multiple uses. I use it as a finish coat to seal and protect my furniture projects. I use both water-based and oil-based polyurethane. I usually use the water-based polyurethane, but if I know a piece will be exposed to lots of water or wear and tear, such as bathroom cabinets or dining room tables, I choose oil-based Arm-R-Seal by Gen-

eral Finishes. Water-based polyurethane by Minwax is clear and very fast drying. I prefer to use a satin finish; it adds just the right amount of shine to give the piece a professional look. Minwax Polycrylic water-based polyurethane is the only clear poly I have found (and I have used every one on the market!) that will not yellow over white, or over any color for that matter.

Shop Towels

Shop towels are my favorite rags to keep on hand. They are sturdy, lint free, superabsorbent, and very soft. You can buy them in rolls or by the box, but either way, they are perfect for cleaning up messes, wiping down furniture, and applying and wiping stains.

Stains

I prefer stains to glazes in my furniture work. Stain is a wood finish that penetrates, seals, and protects with built-in polyurethane. I use stain not only to finish and protect my pieces, but also to add layers of depth and age through application over paint. And I *love* using stain over paint! Stain adds a depth and dimension that softens and blends everything together. A good friend said to me the other day, "Stain on furniture is like a good photo filter." I thought that was a perfect analogy!

I also love stain for the workability time that it gives you and the polished finish that it creates on a painted surface. What do I mean by workability time? Most glazes are acrylic or water based, so they dry very quickly and you do not have much time to move the glaze around; once it's dry, the finish can look a bit forced or unnatural. Stains, however, are oil based and take days to dry completely, so you have plenty of time to make sure that the application is blended and smooth. The only stain I use on my furniture projects is Minwax stain in Special Walnut. I like to keep it simple!

GLUES AND BINDINGS

Double-Sided Mounting Tape

I use mounting tape for holding down paper liners inside furniture drawers. I like to use double-sided mounting tape rather than permanently adhering tape so the paper can be changed out easily. This tape has many other uses, but this is what I use it for in my work.

FrogTape

FrogTape is my masking tape of choice; I truly feel that it is the best on the market. I use FrogTape to mask off all the edges when painting a piece of furniture and to create stripes, custom stencil designs, and dip-dyed patterns on furniture and walls. I believe in having clean, perfectly straight lines when painting. FrogTape ensures a professional finish, and you can purchase it in two formulas: Multi-Surface and Delicate Surface. Frog-Tape Shape Tape is also available in scallop, chevron, and wave patterns so that you can easily create more than just straight lines!

Mod Podge

An all-in-one glue, sealer, and finish, Mod Podge is totally nontoxic, with easy soap-and-water cleanup. Mod Podge is available in several decorative finishes, but I use the matte finish in all of my cut-and-paste projects. You can use Mod Podge in place of wallpaper paste as well if you so choose. Note that if you decide to coat the top of your paper with Mod Podge as a sealer, the surface stays tacky even when dry. To create a smooth surface, I recommend a couple of coats of poly over Mod Podge.

Wood Filler

I use paintable interior wood filler in a natural color to repair small holes, like old hardware holes, scratches, and gouges in wood furniture. Wood filler is easily sanded, painted, and stained, and you can clean it up with soap and water. Apply wood filler with a spackle spatula, and be sure to wipe your tool clean as soon as you are done with your application. If you leave wood filler to dry on a tool, it hardens and renders the tool useless for future projects.

Wood Glue

Wood glue is great for both small and large wood furniture repairs; I choose to use Titebond II Premium wood glue. Wood glue is paintable, sandable, and stainable. If the repair is structural or weight bearing, make sure that you apply the proper clamping and pressure to ensure a proper bond. If the pieces you are gluing are not perfectly aligned, it will affect the outcome and durability of the piece. It is also important to leave the clamps in place for the full drying time specified by the manufacturer.

Belt Sander

A belt sander is stronger than an orbital sander; I use it when I want to remove layers of paint from the surface of a furniture piece or for really heavy sanding jobs that require a bit more power. To achieve a nice smooth surface, work with the grain of the wood and keep the sander constantly moving.

Orbital Sander

I use an orbital sander when preparing a furniture piece for paint, and sometimes for distressing if I want a heavy-handed distressing pattern. The circular motion is gentle on your furniture while at the same time removing any surface irregularities. Keep the sander moving with the grain of the wood. Let the sander do the work for you, and you will have a nice smooth surface in no time.

Craft Knives

I use craft knives for so many projects here at Knack. For lining drawers with paper, it is the best way I have found to get a nice clean edge. I also use a craft knife when applying wallpaper to furniture. I recommend keeping a selection of several different craft knives in different shapes and sizes. The smaller retractable-blade knives are perfect for those tight fits when lining the insides of drawers and when applying wallpaper to furniture. With snap-off blades, you can refresh the blade with each cut, which ensures clean cuts. Larger utility knives are the best choice for the more labor-intensive tasks like cutting through cardboard and trimming veneer.

Rulers and Measuring Tape

Rulers and measuring tapes are two tools that I use daily in my shop. Whether you are marking off guidelines, lining drawers with paper, measuring and cutting wallpaper, or determining the dimensions of a repair/building project, you must have good measuring tools. I use a square ruler by Zona for drawer lining because it fits perfectly in the corner of the drawer. I also use rulers in two sizes: 1 by 12 in/2.5 by 30.5 cm and 36 in/91 cm.

Sanding Sponges

I feel like I can never have too many sanding sponges around the shop! I use sanding sponges in fine and medium grain for all of my hand distressing on furniture. I prefer sanding sponges to sheets of sandpaper simply because they are easy to hold and comfortable to use, and they always produce the kind of distressed finish I'm after.

Long-Nose Pliers with Cutter

I use these pliers for cutting wire and when attaching new hardware to furniture. I can get the bolt only to a certain tightness with my fingers alone, so having a pair of pliers on hand to finish the job is important. The long nose allows great access to small spaces and gives you a firm grip on nuts and bolts when tightening or trying to remove any kind of screw.

Scissors

I keep lots of different pairs of scissors on hand at the shop. I have some kitchen shears that are great for cutting just about anything and other scissors specifically for cutting beautiful papers and wallpapers. Make sure your scissors are sharp.

Squeegee

I have about six or seven of these little guys hanging around at the shop; I use them in Mod Podge paper applications as well as wallpaper applications on furniture. The straight hard surface is the perfect smoothing agent for working out all of the air bubbles under your paper.

3M Stripping Pads

These pads come in very handy when stripping a piece of furniture, especially pieces with grooves, turned legs, and carving details. These pads are hard workers and easily remove paint in those hard-to-reach places that flat hard stripping tools can't get into.

REPAIRS

Clamps

You will need both metal spring clamps and ratchet bar clamps for tightening and gluing furniture pieces. Clamps apply pressure and maintain structure throughout the drying process. I suggest keeping a few different size clamps on hand. Bar clamps are especially useful when gluing and clamping drawers, so be sure to purchase clamps that will extend long enough to fit your drawer size.

Compressor

A compressor is the power source for your nail and staple guns. Using power tools in furniture repair work saves time and energy, plus it is precise. Work smarter, not harder!

Cordless Drill

A cordless drill is essential for drilling new hardware holes, removing old hardware, and tightening up joint screws.

Mask or Respirator

Be sure to wear a mask or respirator when sanding, spray-painting, or applying any chemicals. A dust mask is best for protection during sanding and cleaning. Use a respirator when working with harsh chemicals, using a paint sprayer, or working with spray paint.

Murphy Oil Wood Cleaner

I use this cleaner specifically for cleaning out the inside of furniture pieces before starting work. Most furniture pieces need a good cleaning after purchase. Fill up a bucket of hot water, add the Murphy soap, and give the insides of both the drawers and the furniture a good wipe-down. I love the clean look and smell once I am all done! Do not spray this on the surface of your piece before painting—use it for the insides only.

Nail Gun and Staple Gun

Nail and staple guns are used in conjunction with the compressor. These tools turn bigger jobs—like building a work table, installing new backing on furniture, and making stability repairs—into quick and easy jobs. Nail and staple sizes vary depending on the job; you'll find them at your local hardware store.

Painter's Tool

This is a multipurpose tool that can be used as a putty knife, paint can opener, roller cleaner, hammer, scraper, or spreader; you can even extract nails with it. It's a must-have for anyone in the furniture painting business.

Spackle Spatulas

I use spackle spatulas (also known as "putty knives") for applying wood filler. Use wood filler for smaller repairs like hardware holes, cracks, and scratches. Make sure to clean your putty knives or spatulas well when finished to keep them in smooth working order.

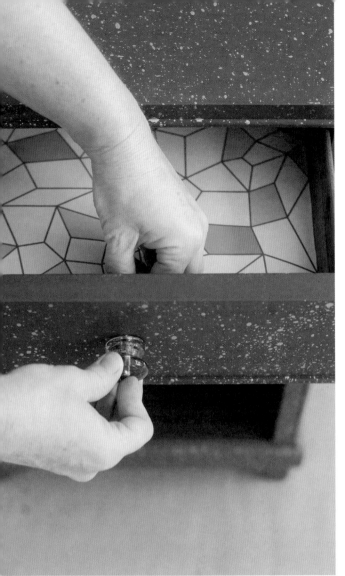

BASIC TECHNIQUES

The following are a few basic techniques to get you started on your furniture projects (you'll find Advanced Techniques starting on page 153). It is important to prep and prepare a piece well for a perfect finish. Details also matter, so take time to line drawers with paper and add new hardware as called for in your designs.

WOOD FILLING

MATERIALS

- - - - - - -

WOOD FILLER, paintable and
stainable

SPACKLE SPATULA

FINE/MEDIUM SANDING SPONGE

SHOP TOWELS

I use wood filler to fill hardware holes in wood furniture
so that I can drill holes to fit new hardware and to fill
shallow nicks and dings in the surface before sanding.

A
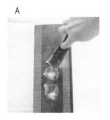

B
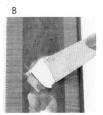

1
A
Fill the hole with wood filler and very lightly smooth over the surface with your spatula. You will be applying the filler twice, so work on getting this first fill as full and smooth as you can get it. Be sure to remove all excess putty surrounding the hole so that it does not create a ridge in your finish or force you to sand through the finish surrounding the hole.

2
Allow the wood filler to dry completely. The deeper the hole, the longer it will take to dry. Shallow fills take 30 minutes to 1 hour to dry; deeper fills may need 3 to 4 hours to dry completely.

3
When the first coat of filler is dry, use the fine/medium sanding sponge to sand it completely smooth before applying the second coat.

4
B
Apply the second coat of filler exactly as you did the first and remove any excess surrounding the repair area. This fill will be very shallow and will dry quickly. You want this fill to be the final fill, so be sure that it is very smooth.

5
When the second fill is dry, sand lightly to make sure it is completely smooth. If you have done the filling correctly, it will not show in your painted finish at all. Wipe down with a shop towel before applying paint.

DISTRESSING

MATERIALS

- - - - - - - -

FINE/MEDIUM SANDING SPONGE

ORBITAL SANDER (optional)

SHOP TOWELS

Proper distressing, using sanders, can make or break a beautiful finish. The goal of distressing is to make the piece look original and timeworn. You want to avoid large, forced markings that draw attention to themselves—and away from the piece.

A
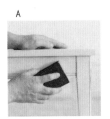

B

C

1   When distressing a piece, start with the hard protruding edges on the tops and sides, as well as any carved detail. Hitting the areas that will get the most wear and tear is a great place to start and creates a natural, timeworn look, as if those places had been rubbed up against for years.

2   I use an orbital sander when I
A   want a heavily distressed paint finish. For all other projects, I use a sanding sponge to achieve a softer distressing pattern.

3   If the piece you are sanding has
B   turned legs and rounded detail, use a sanding sponge and focus on keeping the sponge conformed to the leg and moving consistently over the surface. This technique helps avoid the hard sanding spots that can occur on rounded surfaces that are sanded too harshly.

4   Be careful not to use too much force, as the distressed effect develops pretty easily. Be sure to use long and short strokes when sanding, not circular motions.

5   Sand the entire surface of the
C   piece and wipe down with a shop towel so the surface is uniform and ready for the final finish.

LINING DRAWERS

MATERIALS

- - - - - - - -

VACUUM

WOOD CLEANER

SHOP TOWEL

SCISSORS

RULER

CRAFT KNIFE

WALLPAPER OR WRAPPING PAPER
SHEETS

DOUBLE-SIDED MOUNTING TAPE

Details matter! I line all of the drawers of my furniture pieces with paper because it gives the design a finished look. Papered drawers become a part of the design plan and make opening drawers a treat; it also provides a fresh new surface for storing belongings.

A 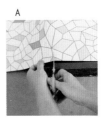   B 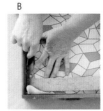   C

1 Vacuum out all of the drawers to remove dust and dirt that may have collected over time. When the entire surface has been vacuumed, clean the inside of the drawers with wood cleaner and a damp shop towel. I use Murphy Oil Soap wood cleaner with orange oil because it not only cleans the wood but also refreshes it and smells wonderful. Be careful not to saturate the wood—just give it a quick wipe-down to clean the surface.

2 Have your scissors, ruler, and craft knife handy. Place the roll of wallpaper beside the drawer, grasp the loose edge, and pull the wallpaper over the top of the drawer. This is the easiest way to measure the length and width that you need for lining the drawer.

3 Use scissors to cut the wallpaper
A to the *outside* measurements of the drawer. This will leave excess once you place the paper inside the drawer, but that is what you want.

4 Place the paper inside the drawer and use one of the straight, uncut edges of the wallpaper as your guide for the front of the drawer. When that guide is in place, use your fingers to smooth the paper and crease it into the other three inner walls of the drawer.

5 Place the ruler against the edge of
B the drawer as tight as you can, still leaving room for the craft knife. Keeping the knife to the right of the ruler at all times, trim the excess paper.

6 When the paper has been
C trimmed to fit the inside of the drawer perfectly, cut four pieces of double-sided mounting tape. Place one piece of tape in each corner of the drawer, and press the paper down onto the tape to hold it securely in place.

ADVANCED TECHNIQUES

These techniques are directly related to the furniture projects in this book. I hope they will provide you with technical know-how necessary to complete your project, as well as inspiration to veer from my process and create something new that best suits your specific furniture piece.

PAINT FLECKING

MATERIALS

- - - - - - - -

SCREWDRIVER OR CORDLESS
DRILL (if needed)

WOOD FILLER (if needed)

FINE/MEDIUM SANDING SPONGE

VACUUM

SHOP TOWELS

DROP CLOTHS

LATEX PAINT

PAINT TRAYS

PAINTBRUSHES

FOAM ROLLER

ROLL OF BROWN KRAFT PAPER

DUCT TAPE

LIQUID GOLD LEAF

PLASTIC GLOVES

CLEAR SEALANT
(for gold leaf)

STAIN (optional)

The way you execute this technique can produce an effect that is either really right or really wrong. If you stand too close to the furniture piece to apply the paint, you will get throw lines in your finish. If you do too much paint splattering, it can look a little sloppy—like DIY gone wrong. I chose a dark gray for the base of this piece and liquid gold leaf for the paint spatters. You can never have too much gold, and the spatter technique adds just the perfect amount of sparkle.

A

B

C

1
A
Remove old hardware using a screwdriver or cordless drill. Fill any old hardware holes with wood filler (see page 150) and allow the wood filler to dry completely before sanding. Sand down the piece with a fine/medium sanding sponge to ensure that it is smooth and ready to accept paint. When finished sanding, measure off and drill your new hardware hole if needed. You can reuse the existing hardware; I usually prefer a fresh new piece of hardware to complete my designs, so I usually have to measure and drill new holes on all of my pieces.

2
B
Vacuum and wipe down the entire piece to remove all dirt and sanding dust. Lay down drop cloths.

3
C
For the base color, paint the furniture piece, using a paintbrush to cut in all of the tight corners and detail areas and a foam roller to roll all of the flat larger surfaces. I applied two coats of paint to this piece with about 2 hours of drying time between coats.

4
Once the paint is dry, you can begin applying your flecks and speckles! This is a messy process, so be sure that you have the work area masked off with either kraft paper or drop cloths and duct tape. I even covered the walls for this one, due to the amount of paint slinging! Take the time to completely protect your work area so you will not be worried about slinging paint where you don't want it.

see Gold-Flecked Side Table
(page 21)

D    E    F    G

TIP:

- - - -

You may want to wear long sleeves and plastic gloves, as the paint-flecking process tends to be messy! I wore gloves, but I wore short sleeves instead of covering my arms, and they had a few extra "freckles" when I was finished!

5 Pour the liquid gold leaf (or desired paint) into a tray. (If your brush is small enough to dip into the jar, by all means go right ahead!) Make sure there is a good amount of paint on the end of your brush—not dripping, but saturated.

6
D Stand 4 to 6 feet back from your piece, loaded paintbrush in hand. This distance is important! If you are too close when you sling the gold leaf, it will create "line" patterns across the furniture. Standing back far enough from the piece ensures that you get a beautiful constellation-type pattern. It is a good idea to test your technique on drop cloths or kraft paper. Practice makes perfect!

7 To fleck, flick your arm, over and over, both vertically and horizontally to ensure even coverage. Turn the piece when you need to start on a new side, and complete each side as you did the first one.

8 Once the flecking pattern is exactly as you like it, let the piece dry completely! Be careful not to smudge your perfect little paint flecks. I allowed my piece to dry overnight.

9
E Once the paint flecks are dry, apply a light coat of stain over the entire piece to seal it and add a little bit of depth. You do not have to add stain, but you will want to use a clear sealant over the liquid gold leaf. Gold leaf needs a sealer to keep it from tarnishing. If you choose to use paint for your flecks, you can seal your piece with stain, wax, or water-based polyurethane.

10
F
G I chose not to sand or distress this piece at all (for once!). You can distress your piece if you wish (see page 151), then wipe it down and vacuum it out, line the drawer with paper (see page 152), and apply the new hardware.

PATCHWORK PAPER

MATERIALS

- - - - - - - -

FINE/MEDIUM SANDING SPONGE

VACUUM

SHOP TOWELS

DROP CLOTHS

MILK PAINT

PURDY 2½-IN/6-CM ANGLED
SASH BRUSH

PAINT CONTAINER (for mixing
and holding the milk paint)

SMALL FOAM PAINTBRUSH

10 TO 12 DIFFERENT SHEETS OF
8½-BY-11-IN/21.5-BY-28-CM
SCRAPBOOK PAPER

SCISSORS

MOD PODGE

SQUEEGEE

CRAFT KNIFE

ORBITAL SANDER

PLASTIC GLOVES

PAINTBRUSH

WATER-BASED POLYURETHANE
STAIN

For paper patchwork, remember to keep your lines as straight as possible so that you can butt your paper edges together. Sometimes this type of decoupage can look a bit messy. That is usually due to lots of overlapped edges, so take the time to do a careful job!

A

B

C

D

1 Sand down your furniture piece with a fine/medium sanding sponge to remove any dirt or loose finish and/or to add some tack to a slick surface.

2 Vacuum and wipe down the entire piece to remove all sanding dust. Make sure the surface is nice and clean before starting to paint and paper. Lay down drop cloths.

3
A Paint the piece. I chose a custom milk paint color (see page 160) and left the top unpainted, since that is where I wanted to apply the patchwork paper. It's okay to paint the surface that you will be papering, but it is not necessary. It can be nice to paint the surface beneath the patchwork if it matches the background of your paper (in case there is any show-through), but go with your preference. Paint the base of the piece with milk paint using the angled sash brush.

4 Once you have completed all the areas you want to be painted and the top surface is dry, start cutting strips of paper and laying out your patchwork design.

5 Continue to cut strips and squares of paper to create different sizes and interesting patchwork. You do not need to measure these strips, but make sure your edges are all nice and straight. Always keep one straight manufactured edge on each piece so you can line it up along the edge of the furniture piece. This way, when you go to line up your patchwork, you can butt the pieces right up next to each other without overlap. This saves having to trim in the end!

6
B
C Apply Mod Podge to both the back of the paper and the furniture surface to ensure a strong adhesion. Be sure to keep your Mod Podge application very smooth so as not to create bubbles under the paper. It is important to not use the Mod Podge in excess, because you want to keep your working surface neat. With practice, you'll learn to use just the right amount.

7
D
E Once the Mod Podge has been applied to both surfaces, place your pieces of paper on the furniture surface in your desired pattern. Smooth out with your hands first and go over the whole

see Patchwork Sofa Table
(page 29)

E

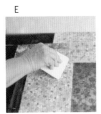

F

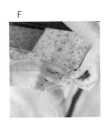

G

H

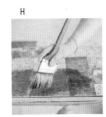

- - - -

Be sure to include variations in both color and pattern in your papers. You want the patchwork to be interesting and not have too many repeats.

- - - -

Scrapbook paper absorbs the Mod Podge and becomes soft while it is wet. Cutting this type of paper while wet will create a rough, torn mess. With this type of paper, it is critical to wait until the paper is dry before you trim. However, if you are using a thicker coated paper or wallpaper for your project, you can trim the paper immediately.

- - - -

Any sections where Mod Podge has been wiped on top of the paper will take the stain differently at first. I actually welcome this look, but if you do not care for it, just coat the entire paper surface with Mod Podge before applying the stain, and the stain will be absorbed evenly. Stain, being oil based, will seep and spread as it dries, but as it dries, it will eventually settle and appear more uniform. When the surface is not perfect, it makes the piece look genuinely timeworn. I learned this from years of experimenting with finishes and paper. I have even poured acetone on spots after the stain was applied to create color variance and an aged look in the paper! Think of the paper surface as a canvas—the more layers of Mod Podge, stain, and poly you can create and add, the more rich and intriguing it gets.

surface with a squeegee. Wipe away any excess Mod Podge that seeps out onto the surface of the paper with a clean shop towel. If you are too carefree and messy, it may come back to haunt you in the staining process (see step 13).

8 Keep applying pieces of cut paper to the surface until you reach the edge of the furniture piece. I line up as many straight edges of the paper with the straight edges of the furniture piece as I can.

9
F With this sofa table, the edges were a bit rounded, so when a square of paper was added to the rounded edge, there was a bit of an overlap. If this happens, let the paper dry and then go back and use a craft knife to trim the paper edges for a clean fit.

10
G Once you have applied all of the patchwork paper, let it dry completely, and trimmed it, you can begin sanding. I chose to use an orbital sander on this surface since I wanted to create a timeworn look. Be careful when using an orbital sander on paper! You have to work on each section very briefly, with a light touch, to avoid making your paper disappear. Using a sander around the edges also helps remove any excess overlap you may not have gotten with trimming.

11 If, while sanding, you see that a few edges of your paper are loose or have lifted, put some Mod Podge on a small paintbrush and paint over the edge to secure it back down.

12 When you are done sanding, vacuum and wipe down the surface with a shop towel to remove all sanding dust.

13
H Now you can apply the finish. I used two different finishes on this piece: a water-based polyurethane over the milk painted base, and a stain over the papered top to create age and depth, for a timeworn look. You will need to use a different paintbrush for each finish, since you are dealing with both oil-based and water-based products. Since I used a very porous unsealed paper for this project, the stain altered the colors and look of the paper significantly when applied. This was an intentional move on my part, but if you are not prepared for it, it can be a bit unsettling! If you do not want your paper to change in any way and you have used a porous gift-wrap or scrapbook paper for your project, apply several coats of water-based polyurethane to seal the paper before applying any other type of finish.

SPRAY-PAINT GRAFFITI

MATERIALS

- - - - - - - -

FINE/MEDIUM SANDING SPONGE

VACUUM

SHOP TOWELS

FROGTAPE (optional, for masking off drawers and areas that you want to keep free of spray paint)

DROP CLOTHS

SPRAY PAINT, in six to eight colors

CARDBOARD PIECES (to create straight lines)

STENCILS

LIQUID GOLD LEAF

WHITE PAINT PEN

PLASTIC GLOVES

ORBITAL SANDER

MINWAX SPECIAL WALNUT STAIN

PURDY CHINA SERIES BRUSH

WALLPAPER (optional for drawer lining)

Who doesn't love a good, cathartic graffiti installation? For the Graffiti Desk, I worked with multiple jewel-toned colors of spray paint, stencils, and liquid gold leaf to make a layered work of art. Go at it solo or do the project with a group of friends.

  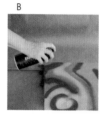 

A · B · C

1 Prep your furniture by lightly sanding the entire piece with a fine/medium sanding sponge, then vacuum and wipe down with a slightly damp shop towel to remove all sanding dust.

2 Remove the existing hardware, for painting later, and tape off drawer tops, sides, and any other areas that you want to keep free of paint overspray. Lay down drop cloths.

3
A
Begin by spray-painting a base coat on the entire furniture piece in several different colors. This is not the design part yet; you are simply creating a colorful, even base for your design.

4
B
C
When the base coat is complete and dry, start spray-painting layers of design in whatever pattern and form that you like. Use elements that are meaningful and important to you: letters, numbers, symbols, and words. I chose to use pieces of cardboard boxes to create angles and straight lines as well as cardboard stencils of letters and numbers to make the execution a little bit easier, but you can freehand everything if you prefer. Relax and enjoy yourself: the beautiful thing about creating graffiti is that if you "mess up," you can just spray over it and start again. The more layers you have, the better.

5 When you have covered the entire piece with paint and are happy with the overall look, and the surface is dry, go in and create some detail. I chose to use liquid gold leaf to create splatters and a white paint pen to create random geometric patterns. I achieved the gold splatters by putting on plastic gloves, dipping my fingers in gold leaf, and flicking drops onto the piece.

see Graffiti Desk
(page 37)

D   E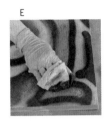

6   Spray-paint your hardware or get
     new hardware ready. I chose to
     keep the existing hardware on
     this piece, but I spray-painted it
     in one of the green colors that
     we used on the desk. Painting the
     hardware a solid color gave the
     piece a polished look and is a nice
     grounding element.

7   With so many paint layers and
  D spray paint, a good sanding is
     needed. I used an orbital sander
     to sand the entire piece down and
     smooth out any rough areas. This
     did not cause distressing, because
     I worked fast and I had layered a
     lot of paint on the piece, but you
     can distress the surface if you like
     (see page 151).

8   When you are finished sanding,
     vacuum and wipe down the entire
     piece with a damp shop towel to
     remove all sanding dust.

9   Apply Minwax stain in Special
  E Walnut with a Purdy China
     Series brush, one section at a
     time, wiping immediately after
     application.

10   Once the stain is dry to the
     touch, usually after about
     48 hours, line the drawers with
     paper (see page 152) and attach
     the hardware!

TIPS:

- - - -

Make sure you are working in a
well-ventilated area when using
spray paint. If the ventilation
is not good, wear a respirator
to protect yourself.

- - - -

Make sure you are working in an
area that you can make a mess in,
and use plenty of drop cloths!

- - - -

Practice a light touch on the
spray can to create thinner
lines and designs. If you press
the nozzle all the way down, you
will create large splotches and
have less control. Also, keep
the can moving at all times to
help control the flow of paint.

APPLYING MILK PAINT

MATERIALS

- - - - - - - -

MEASURING CUP (large enough
to hold 3 cups/720 ml)

MILK PAINT

HOT WATER

STIR STICK

120-GRIT FINE SANDING SPONGE

VACUUM

SHOP TOWELS

DROP CLOTHS

PURDY NYLOX 2½-IN/6-CM
ANGLED SASH BRUSH (for the
milk paint)

HAIR DRYER (for crackling)

MINWAX POLYCRYLIC SATIN
POLYURETHANE

PURDY WHITE BRISTLE BRUSH

Milk paint has long been one of my favorite paints to work with because it is so user-friendly and easy to apply. Milk paint creates a timeworn, authentic look that cannot be achieved using any other paint. Even though milk paint application does require some care and skill, the end result appears effortless and natural. There is no forced distressing, as milk paint distresses on its own. The result is an appearance of age and depth acquired over time. The wood on this old church pew soaked up the milk paint like a sponge and turned out beautifully. I mixed my own custom gray color using both black and white milk paint until I achieved the tone I was looking for. This is another wonderful property of milk paint—you can create your own custom color line!

A

B

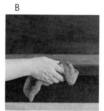

C

1
A
Start by mixing the paint. The consistency of milk paint tends to be like pancake batter; once mixed, it needs to sit for a little bit to "set up," so I like to mix the paint and let it sit while I get the furniture ready to go. Mixing milk paint with hot water rather than cold water helps the powder and water come together. Use a stir stick to stir, and stir some more! Milk paint requires a lot of mixing. You don't need any fancy mixing tools—a stir stick works just fine—but if you have mixing whisks, by all means use them.

2
Prep the furniture piece by lightly sanding it. I recommend sanding with a fine sanding sponge simply to create a nice porous surface for the paint. Sanding also removes dirt and grime—a necessary part of creating a nice clean painting surface.

3
B
When you are finished sanding the piece, vacuum it to remove all of the sanding dust, then wipe it down with a slightly damp shop towel. These steps ensure a nice clean surface, ready for paint. Lay down drop cloths.

see Milk Paint Pew
(page 45)

D E  F

4
C
Apply the first coat of milk paint with the angled sash brush, stroking with the wood grain whenever possible. I do not recommend using a foam roller to apply milk paint; it does not work with the consistency of milk paint and leaves a textured finish. Part of the beauty of milk paint is the hand-applied look, and in this instance some brush marks actually add to the beauty of the final finish.

5 Milk paint dries extremely fast, so begin applying the second coat as soon as the first coat is completely dry. (Just be careful not to apply the second coat too soon, as it will cause the first coat to come off.) If your milk paint has gotten a bit thick during drying time, just add a tiny bit more hot water and give it a few good stirs.

6 When applying the second coat of milk paint, apply it heavily in the areas where you'd like to create a crackling effect.

7
D
Immediately after applying the second coat, use a hair dryer on the thick wet sections of paint. Under the hot air from the hair dryer, the milk paint dries very quickly and begins to crack in a beautiful way.

8
E
Once the second coat of paint is completely dry and you have a crackled look that you like, sand down the entire piece to distress, if you wish (see page 151) and to remove any loose paint.

9 Vacuum the entire piece to remove all sanding dust, and wipe down with a *dry* shop towel. Milk paint is very dry and porous before it is sealed, so do not use a wet towel on it at this time.

10
F
Apply two or three coats of water-based Minwax Polycrylic Satin Polyurethane for finish and protection. I use a Purdy White Bristle brush for all of my polyurethane applications. The bristles are a bit softer and don't create brush strokes in the finish. Water-based polyurethane dries pretty quickly, so you may only need to wait about 30 minutes between coats, depending on the temperature and environment in which you are painting.

OMBRÉ LETTERING

MATERIALS

- - - - - - - -

FINE SANDING SPONGE

VACUUM

SHOP TOWELS

DROP CLOTHS

FOAM ROLLERS (one for each paint color)

PAINT (I used three blue colors for the lettering, plus white)

PAINT TRAYS (one for each paint color)

PLASTIC-COATED ALPHABET STICKERS (do *not* use porous paper stickers)

RULER (optional)

PURDY NYLOX 2½-IN/6-CM ANGLED SASH BRUSH

SMALL ARTIST PAINTBRUSH (for touchups)

ORBITAL SANDER (optional)

PLASTIC GLOVES

MINWAX SPECIAL WALNUT STAIN

PURDY WHITE BRISTLE BRUSH

I am a lover of words and quotes, and I post at least one on my blog every week. My husband is a graphic designer as well, so we are just big fans of typography and print. I really enjoy being able to combine that love of typography with furniture design, and this lettering technique is a perfect example of when two loves collide to create a winning combination. The technique is essentially a "reverse mask": you first paint the piece with an ombré of your chosen lettering colors, then apply the quote with waterproof letter stickers, paint a topcoat over these, and finally remove the stickers to reveal the quote.

A

B

C

1 Prep your piece before painting by lightly sanding, then vacuuming, and wiping down with a damp shop towel. Lay down drop cloths.

2 Using a foam roller for each color, paint on the base colors that you want for the letters. For the Quote Coffee Table, I chose Blue Danube by Benjamin Moore and then custom lightened it into two additional shades of blue by mixing in White Dove, also by Benjamin Moore. You can customize your own colors or simply use a paint chip and pick three consecutive color tones ranging from dark to light.

3 I used the width of the foam roller as my guide when applying the three blue colors and free-handed the ombré application. Do not tape off your lines; if you do, the buildup around the tape line will show through your final finish. Apply two coats of each color, allowing proper drying time between coats.

4
A
B
When the base colors for your letters are completely dry, apply your quote using plastic-coated alphabet stickers. Depending on the furniture piece you are using, the application may be a bit different, but the steps will be the same. For my design, I chose an off-center application and used the straight edge of the coffee table as a guide. I tend to eye things rather than actually measuring with a ruler. Use whatever method you trust most.

5
C
Once all of your stickers are in place, apply the topcoat of paint over the entire piece of furniture. For the coffee table, I chose white as a topcoat because I really

see Quote Coffee Table
(page 53)

D

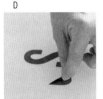

E

F

G

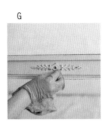

wanted the darker colors underneath to pop. Don't feel like you can use only white as a topcoat. Experiment with the colors you like the best, but just make sure there is enough contrast between the topcoat and bottom colors. Using a brush to cut in all of the tight spaces and a foam roller to roll all of the flat surfaces, apply two thin coats of paint with ample drying time in between each coat. Be careful not to pile on the paint, especially around your letters. If too much paint pools around the letters it will bubble and peel off when you remove the stickers.

6
D When the second coat of paint is completely dry, remove the letter stickers. This is different from the FrogTape technique, in which we remove the tape as soon as the second coat of paint has been applied. If you try to remove these stickers while the paint is wet, it creates a huge mess and you will have lots of touch-ups to do. (I speak from experience!)

7 Ideally all of your letters will come off smoothly, but you may end up with a rough or uneven edge. No worries—just use your paint colors and a small artist paintbrush to touch up as needed.

8
E For the piece on page 53, I chose to complete the design with a heavy distress (see page 151) and Special Walnut stain. I sanded the entire piece down, achieving really rough distressed patches that I think contrast beautifully with the white finish. If you'd like to take either of these optional steps, wait until the lettering design is completely dry (and touched up, if necessary), then proceed.

9 Use an orbital sander to distress the piece as much or little as you wish.

10 Once the sanding is complete, vacuum and then wipe down the entire piece with a slightly damp shop towel to remove all sanding dust.

11
F
G For the final step, apply Minwax Special Walnut stain with a Purdy White Bristle brush. Apply the stain in sections, making sure to coat the entire section. As you complete each section, use a clean shop towel to immediately wipe and blend in the stain to your liking. You can leave the stain on for up to 5 minutes, but keep in mind that the longer it is on, the darker it will get.

12 Let dry completely. Stain can stay tacky for up to 48 hours, so be sure to keep the piece in a clean, dust-free environment until it is completely dry.

CUSTOM FROGTAPE STENCILING

MATERIALS

- - - - - - - -

DROP CLOTHS

LATEX PAINT (in several colors)

PAINT TRAYS

FOAM ROLLER

PURDY NYLOX 2½-IN/6-CM ANGLED SASH BRUSH

FROGTAPE

RULER

CRAFT KNIFE

FINE SANDING SPONGE

SHOP TOWELS

PLASTIC GLOVES

MINWAX SPECIAL WALNUT STAIN

PURDY CHINA SERIES BRUSH

VACUUM

WALLPAPER (optional, to line the drawers)

You may think that FrogTape is only for ensuring straight lines and keeping your trim nice and neat when painting a room. Both of those are really great uses, but you can also create custom templates and stencils with this tape. The possibilities are endless! I decided to try an abstract city skyline design on this dresser, and I love the way it turned out.

A	B	C	D
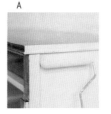		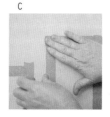	

1
A
B
Lay down drop cloths. Paint your furniture piece with the base color, using a foam roller for all of the large flat surfaces and an angled sash paintbrush for cutting in the tight spots. Apply two coats of paint on the entire piece and let it dry completely before applying any tape designs. I recommend waiting at least 24 hours to make sure the base coat is nice and stable.

2
C
Begin taping off your design. (With a freehand design like the city skyline, you don't have to map out the entire design before you start. You are using tape, so it can easily be adjusted as you go along.) Tear off the first piece of tape and place it at the starting point of your design. I chose to wrap the design around both the front and sides of this piece.

3 Keep adding straight lines of tape until you start to see the city skyline (or whatever your design is) forming. Get really creative here, and create wide, thin, tall, and short shapes that will give your design lots of movement. As you tear or cut off the tape to place it on the piece and create your design, there may be places where you need to go in and create a clean straight line (instead of a torn edge). Use your ruler and craft knife to score places in your tape that need to be removed, but be careful not to push too hard and create scratch lines in your paint finish.

4
D
Once the entire design is taped, pour paint into a tray and begin painting within the taped areas. I used a roller and a brush in this application, since the surface is really flat. Feel free to use whichever combination of tools best suits the surface you are working on.

see City Skyline Dresser
(page 61)

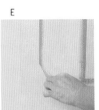

E

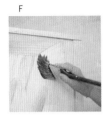

F

5   After the first coat dries (1 to
2 hours), apply a second coat of
paint exactly as you did the first.

6   Once the second coat of paint has
E   been applied, immediately remove
the tape before the paint dries.

7   Once the paint is dry, you may want
to sand and distress the piece (see
page 151); this is optional. I chose to
very lightly distress just a few edges,
but I left the flat surfaces nice and
smooth. Be sure to wipe the piece
down before applying stain.

8   Apply the stain to your piece with
F   a Purdy China Series brush. I chose
to apply stain over paint for the
City Skyline Dresser. You could
also use a clear satin water-based
polyurethane.

9   Vacuum and wipe down your
piece of furniture, install the new
hardware, and line the drawers
with paper (see page 152). If you
do not have wallpaper to line the
drawers, you can paint the insides
of the drawers instead. There are
such creative ways to make drawers
appealing and artful, so get creative!

TIPS:

- - - -

Apply the paint in light coats!
Less is more, especially when
painting around tape. Keep the
bulk of your paint in the center
of the taped-off design and
gently work it out toward the
edges of the tape line with your
brush or roller. This ensures
that the lighter coats of paint
will be near the edges of the
tape. Excess paint near the edge
of the tape can sometimes get
underneath the tape and cause
unsightly bleed marks. These can
be fixed, but we want to keep
the lines as perfect as possible
on the first try!

- - - -

When removing FrogTape, always
pull it toward the painted line
rather than away from it. This
helps keep pressure off of the
paint line and keeps it nice
and smooth.

WEATHERING WITH PAINT

MATERIALS

- - - - - - - -

VACUUM

SHOP TOWELS

DROP CLOTHS

PAINT (several colors)

PAINT TRAYS

PAINTBRUSHES

FOAM ROLLERS

BELT SANDER

MEDIUM-GRIT SANDPAPER BELT
(for belt sander)

ORBITAL SANDER

FINE-GRIT SANDPAPER PAD
(for orbital sander)

ARM-R-SEAL OIL-BASED
POLYURETHANE

PURDY CHINA SERIES BRUSH

MINERAL SPIRITS

When applying multiple colors of paint, covering with a single-color topcoat, and then using a belt sander to reveal the hidden colors, it helps if the wood is super porous and a bit rough. A belt sander is a powerful tool and quickly eats through layers, so the tough and porous wood takes the sanding well. When you're done weathering, you have a really smooth and beautiful table that is ready to serve you in the kitchen, act as a desk in the living room, or help out at your next outdoor party.

A  B  C

1 Since this table is going to get
a lot of sanding, vacuum first to
remove dust, dirt, cobwebs, and
loose wood splinters, then wipe
down with a slightly damp shop
towel. Lay down drop cloths.

2 Using as many colors as you
A want, start applying paint with
a paintbrush in random abstract
patterns all over the surface of
the tabletop. Do not layer colors
on top of each other; paint indi-
vidual sections different colors.
The colors can overlap a bit since
the design is freehand. Cover the
entire top in color and let it dry
(1 to 2 hours).

3 Once the tabletop is dry, apply
B the topcoat. (I chose a really pale
C gray for my topcoat. You can use
white instead—or any other color
you want—but I feel that using a
light topcoat creates a stronger
"weathered" look and a more uni-
fied design.) Use a foam roller for
a nice smooth coat of paint over
the various colors.

4 Let the first topcoat dry for about
1 hour, then apply a second topcoat exactly as you did the first.

5 When the paint is good and dry,
D begin the sanding process. Start
sanding with a medium-grit sanding
belt over the entire surface, going
with the wood grain. Remember
that a belt sander is very powerful
and will remove paint easily, so
keep the sander moving and be
careful not to press down too hard.
Let the sander do the work!

see Weathered Dining Table
(page 69)

D   E

 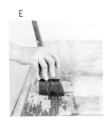

6   After the belt sanding is done, take an orbital sander with a fine sanding pad attached and give the entire top an additional sanding. This removes the coarseness left behind by the belt sander. Going from medium to fine with the sanding paper produces a nice smooth surface.

7   When all of the sanding is finished, vacuum the entire surface to remove all sanding dust. Wipe down the entire piece with a slightly damp shop towel to catch any remaining dust.

8
E   Apply three coats of oil-based polyurethane, using a Purdy China Series paintbrush and allowing 3 to 5 hours of drying time between coats. I highly recommend General Finishes Arm-R-Seal; it's the only oil polyurethane I use.

9   Once the oil-based topcoat is good and dry, your table is ready to use!

TIPS:

- - - -

A belt sander works best on flat surfaces. Do not use it on any carved or turned detail; it will ruin the detail and therefore ruin the piece.

- - - -

For this piece, I wanted most of the bare wood to show through, with patches of paint remaining here and there. Yes, you'll be sanding off most of the paint you've applied—both colors and topcoat—with the belt sander, leaving only patches of paint. If you want to preserve more of the paint, sand until the patterns and ratios of paint to natural wood are just to your liking.

DRESSER INTO A BOOKCASE

MATERIALS

- - - - - - - -

HAMMER OR MALLET AND CHISEL

SPACKLE SPATULA

FLAT-HEAD SCREWDRIVER

PLYWOOD SHELVING

WOOD FILLER

NAILS

DROP CLOTHS

MILK PAINT

PLASTIC MEASURING CUP
(to mix milk paint in)

LATEX PAINT

PAINT TRAYS

2 PURDY 2½-IN/6-CM ANGLED
SASH BRUSHES

FOAM ROLLERS

FINE SANDING SPONGE

VACUUM

SHOP TOWELS

FURNITURE WAX

WAX BRUSH

It seems like antique bookcases with interesting shapes and detail have been pushed aside for the utilitarian designs produced by the big box retailers. So when I saw this tall chest of drawers with the beautiful wide base and then realized that the bottom drawer unit was damaged, I knew it would be a perfect candidate for creating a bookcase, since we needed to remove the drawers to create a bookcase anyway. The drawers were deep and wide on the bottom, and by removing a drawer in the middle of the dresser, we created some additional space and shelving. Because turning this piece into a bookcase required a bit more carpentry skill than I possess, I enlisted the help of my carpenter friend Steve.

A   B   C   D

1
A — Remove the back panel for easier access to both the front and rear of the piece. To do this, use a hammer or mallet and a chisel to pry the back away from the sides and shelves and continue all the way around until completely loosened, then set it aside.

2
B
C — Use a screwdriver to remove the drawer runners. (We did this because we were installing a plywood shelf at that point and wanted the surface to be nice and flat.) Use a screwdriver or spackle spatula to pry up the drawer stoppers as well.

3 On my piece, I decided to remove one of the middle drawer slots to create more space. You may like where the drawers in your piece are located; if so, you don't have to change anything. If you do want to change it, figure out how you want your bookshelves to be spaced and, if necessary, remove

any existing framework now. Just make sure that the piece of furniture will remain structurally sound after you remove the drawer slot.

4 Once you have the spaces created and the plan for the shelves in place, add the new plywood shelving. (With my project, the shelves were made to be flush with the existing drawer structure and then screwed in from the outside of the piece. The screws were counter sunk and then wood filler was used to cover and smooth over the holes.)

5 When all of the shelves are placed, nail the back panel back on. The piece is now ready for painting! Lay down drop cloths.

6
D
E — Cut in all the corners and edges with one of your Purdy angled sash brushes, then roll all of the flat shelves and surfaces with a foam roller. (I chose to paint the outside of this piece with

see Bookcase Dresser
(page 77)

E
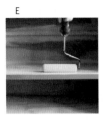

F

G

TIP:

- - - -

Keep a wet shop towel on hand
to wipe any edges clean as you
paint. When you apply the outside
coat of milk paint, you may
find that some paint creeps onto
the color on the inside of the
cabinet. Since the interior paint
is latex, you can easily wipe it
off with a wet shop towel—just
do it right away. This may seem
tedious, but it is important that
the paint finish comes out neat.

a pumpkin-colored milk paint because I wanted the timeworn and washed look. I painted the inside with a really pale pink latex to give it a smooth modern finish. I like this combination of textures; it gives the piece interest and depth. If you go with two colors, paint the inside shelving of the bookcase first. Wait for the latex paint on the inside to dry, usually about 2 hours, before painting the outside of the piece.)

7   If you choose to use milk paint, brush two coats on the outside of the bookcase with a fresh Purdy angled sash brush (see Applying Milk Paint, page 160). Milk paint dries pretty fast, so you will need to wait only about 1 hour to apply the second coat.

8   Once the second coat of milk paint
F   is nice and dry, it is time to sand. Using a fine sanding sponge, very lightly sand all of the hard edges on the outside of the piece. I did not sand the inside shelving because I wanted it to remain a solid color, and I did not do a heavy distress on this piece.

9   When you are finished distressing, lightly vacuum the entire piece to remove all sanding dust. Then wipe down the piece with a dry shop towel to remove any remaining dust.

10 I chose a wax finish for this piece
G   because a wax finish over milk paint is really subtle and easy to apply, gives a really pretty muted shine, and tends to deepen the paint color just a bit. To apply, dip your wax brush in the wax and scrape the edge of the brush against the rim of the wax container to evenly distribute the wax on the bristles. Be careful not to get heavy handed; with wax, less is more, so don't overload the brush; it's better to dip again frequently.

11 With the wax distributed evenly on the brush, apply it to the piece exactly as you would paint. Going with the grain of wood, make long, even strokes that overlap just the tiniest bit on each pass. Apply the wax to all surfaces of the piece.

12 Finally, buff the wax. Wax dries very fast—you can start buffing as early as 30 minutes after application— but you can wait longer. I usually let a piece sit overnight to let the wax set up and get a little bit hard; then I buff it out with a dry shop towel. If you decide to buff out the wax sooner rather than later, just keep an eye out for streaks. If you feel like you are rubbing and rubbing only to find more blurriness and streaks, stop and give the wax more time to dry.

13 Once the wax is all dry and buffed, your bookcase is ready to be filled with treasures!

SCALLOPED DIP-DYEING

MATERIALS

- - - - - - - -

FINE SANDING SPONGES

VACUUM

SHOP TOWELS

FROGTAPE SHAPE TAPE IN
SCALLOP

CRAFT KNIFE

RULER

SQUEEGEE

FROGTAPE MULTI-SURFACE TAPE

DROP CLOTHS

PAINT

PAINT TRAY

PURDY 2½-IN/6-CM ANGLED
SASH BRUSH

FOAM ROLLER

MINWAX SPECIAL WALNUT STAIN

PURDY CHINA SERIES BRUSH

Painting furniture is my passion, but there are times when I like to leave a little glimpse of the natural wood showing through. Taping off and creating a dip-dye look is the perfect way to join the painted and nonpainted surfaces. For this particular piece, instead of just creating a straight line of demarcation, I chose to make it a bit more playful and created a soft scalloped edge.

A

B

C

D

1 Lightly sand, vacuum, and wipe down the entire piece of furniture with a damp shop towel so that it is nice and clean and ready to accept paint. Remove hardware at this time as well. I chose new hardware for this piece, but the existing holes were exactly as they needed to be for the new hardware. If this is not the case, you will need to wood fill and drill new holes for your new hardware now (see Wood Filling on page 150).

2 Figure out where you want the scallop paint line to be. (I wanted the line to be about one-quarter of the way up from the bottom of the piece so the richness of the wood remained visible, but not too much.)

3 Apply the tape to the piece, work-
A ing from left to right. I started on the left side, wrapping the tape around to the front and then back around the right side. If you feel more confident working in separate sections for each side, do so; just make sure the scallops align properly at the overlapping points. Use a craft knife and ruler when trimming the edges so the tapeline remains straight. I do not measure, but you can! I find that my eye is better than a ruler sometimes.

4 When the scallop tape line is all in
B place, use a squeegee to go over the entire tape line. This ensures that the tape is adhered and will keep your paint lines sharp.

see Scalloped Sideboard
(page 85)

E

F

G

H

5 Once the scallop tape line is in place, use the FrogTape Multi-Surface tape to mask off all of the drawer sides and runners to keep the exterior paint lines nice and straight. Lay down drop cloths.

6 Apply the first coat of paint to the
C exterior. Use a Purdy 2½-in/6-cm angled sash brush first to cut in all the crevices, corners, and areas where a roller will not reach; then immediately roll the same surfaces to blend the cut-in lines and make sure the finish is perfectly smooth. Be careful not to paint under your tape line, and do not apply paint thickly near the tape, as this will cause a buildup around the edge and create issues when you remove the tape. Always blend and manipulate paint while it is wet! It is the only chance you get to ensure a nice smooth finish.

7 Allow the first coat of paint to dry
D (1 to 2 hours, or until no longer tacky feeling) and apply a second coat exactly as you did the first. As soon as you complete the second coat, immediately remove the scallop tape.

8 When the second coat of paint is
E dry, you can either leave the finish as is or you can distress it a bit. (On my piece, I used a fine sanding sponge to distress the finish just a tiny bit around the edges and hard lines to create some interest in the finish.)

9 When you are finished sanding, vacuum off the sanding dust before applying the stain.

10 Use the Purdy China Bristle brush
F to apply the stain directly onto the
G piece of furniture. I applied the stain to the entire piece, both the painted and unpainted surfaces, which helped unify the look. There is no single correct pattern; you want to make sure the entire surface is covered evenly. The longer the stain sits on the surface, the darker it will become. If you would like it a bit darker, leave it on for up to 5 minutes. Otherwise, as soon as the stain has been applied to a section you can immediately use a dry shop towel to wipe the stain off. Wipe exactly as you painted, going with the grain of the wood and making sure that the stain appears blended and not smudgy.

11 Allow the stain to dry completely
H for 2 to 3 days. Then you can line the drawers (see page 152) and attach the new hardware! I lined the drawers with a gorgeous vintage leaf wallpaper, gifted to me by a friend.

TIPS:

- - - -

When applying the scallop tape, be careful not to pull and stretch it. Stretching causes strain on the tape and will distort the scalloped design. Use minimal pressure and work in manageable sections so you can be sure that your line is nice and straight.

- - - -

The paint blocker in the tape is activated by water, so if you are taping off an unpainted piece of furniture (like mine was), *after* you use the squeegee to make sure the tape is fully adhered, wipe over the entire tape line with a damp shop towel to activate the seal.

APPLYING DECALS

MATERIALS

- - - - - - - -

FINE SANDING SPONGE

VACUUM

SHOP TOWELS

DROP CLOTHS

PAINT

PAINT TRAYS

PURDY 2½-IN/6-CM ANGLED
SASH BRUSH

FOAM ROLLER

MINWAX WATER-BASED SATIN
POLYURETHANE

PURDY CHINA SERIES BRUSH

WALL DECALS (feathers,
in this design)

SQUEEGEE

I decided on a falling feather pattern down the front of this piece. Applying decals is a really great way to add an intentional artistic detail to a piece. I purchased these feathers at Target; they are actually wall decals, but they work well on furniture too. The most crucial part of applying decals is execution. Be creative with the placement of your decals so that they elevate the piece. If you want to paper the front of the drawers to complete the look of this armoire design, turn to page 181.

 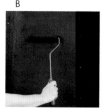  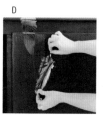

A · B · C · D

1
A You may notice in the "before" photo that this piece had a fleur-type design carved on the front of the doors. I decided to cover that design using wood filler (see page 150) because I felt like it dated the piece. If you have a similar detail you want to eliminate this way, be sure to apply only where the fill is needed, and keep the filler nice and smooth.

2 Remove existing hardware, lightly sand the entire piece with a fine sanding sponge, vacuum, and wipe down with a damp shop towel to make sure the piece is clean and ready for paint. Lay down drop cloths.

3
B Apply the first coat of paint, using an angled sash brush to cut in all of the trim and edges where the roller cannot reach. Work in one section at a time and roll the flat surfaces immediately after

cutting in with a brush. Overlap the brushed line just a bit to make sure that the finish is nice and smooth. Allow this first coat to dry.

4
C Apply a second coat of paint just like the first. I decided to paint the inside of this piece as well—it's a nice detail that makes the piece look polished. I also chose to wallpaper the drawer fronts (see page 181) to add more detail and unexpected surprise upon opening the doors. It matters!

5 When the second coat of paint has dried (usually about 2 hours), it is time to apply the polyurethane finish (see Tip). Pour the polyurethane into a paint tray or plastic container and use a Purdy China Series brush to apply. Make sure there is ample polyurethane on your brush, and make one pass per section, overlapping the previous section the tiniest bit to make

see Feather Decal Armoire
(page 93)

E

F

sure that the surface is covered completely. Work with the grain of the wood exactly as you painted. Work in long, even strokes and try to span the entire surface in one stroke if you can. This helps to avoid brush marks and patterns in your finish.

6 Let the first coat of polyurethane dry (1 to 2 hours). If you see some uneven places or brush marks, lightly sand the entire surface and vacuum up the dust. Then apply the second coat exactly as you did the first.

7 When the second coat of polyure-thane is dry (1 to 2 hours), plan out your decal design. Do you want it asymmetrical, centered, uniform, random? Wall decals are made to be removable, but they are quite sticky, so I highly recommend placing them right the first time.

8 Peel each decal from its paper
<u>D</u> backing and place it where you
<u>E</u> want it on the piece. Smooth and work out any air bubbles with your hand first and then give it a good going-over with the squeegee.

9 Continue to add decals exactly as
<u>F</u> you did the first until you feel like your design is complete.

TIPS:

- - - -

Polyurethane can be really difficult to apply over dark colors, so it is important to do it right. Water-based polyurethane dries superfast, and you absolutely must not work it too much or you will have streaks and smudges in your finish. I try to turn off my air-conditioning when I apply this stuff because even that bit of air movement can dry a finish fast.

- - - - -

We applied the feather decals *after* the polyurethane finish because the decals are made to be removable—so if you tire of the decal design, you can easily change it. If you apply polyurethane over the feathers, it makes it difficult to remove them—you would have to sand and repaint the piece where the feathers were placed.

STRIPPING PAINT

- - - - - - - -

PAPER OR PLASTIC DROP CLOTHS

CHEMICAL-RESISTANT GLOVES

CITRISTRIP

PLASTIC CONTAINER OR PAINT
TRAY FOR CITRISTRIP

PAINTBRUSH (for applying
Citristrip; this can be a
cheap throwaway brush)

PAINTER'S TOOL (for scraping
the paint off)

MINERAL SPIRITS

METAL OR PLASTIC BUCKET (to
pour mineral spirits into)

STRIPPING PADS

SHOP TOWELS

FINE SANDING SPONGE

VACUUM

DANISH OIL

Stripping a piece of furniture is a gooey, messy job! It is not difficult, but it can be tedious and time consuming. This chair had four layers of paint on it, so it took a few days of working in 3- to 4-hour spurts to get all of the paint off and get the surface of the wood nice and clean. Trust me, the result is always worth the time and effort. I chose to keep this piece natural wood and not paint it (crazy, right?), so I just used Danish oil on the wood to seal it.

A

B

1 Lay plastic or paper on the ground underneath your project, or work on the project outside where you can make a mess. Remove any fabric trim or upholstery that will be in the way or compromise the final finish. Make sure that all of the wood can be stripped completely and is not hidden by upholstery trim. If you do not tear the trim off, the upholsterer will, and if you have not stripped underneath the existing trim, you will have to go back and do it. Nobody wants to do that!

2 Put on your chemical-resistant gloves and pour some Citristrip into a paint tray or plastic container.

3 Apply the Citristrip to the wood
A with a throwaway brush. Cover the entire surface with a thick coating so that it can stay nice and wet while it starts to work. It is best to work with Citristrip while it is wet; thankfully, Citristrip starts to work pretty quickly.

4 When you see the paint start to
B bubble, it is time to start gently removing it with the painter's tool. With Citristrip, you should not have to scrape hard at all; the paint will just peel right off. Remove as much of the bubbled loose paint as possible before applying a second coat of Citristrip.

see Stripped Indigo Chair
(page 101)

C 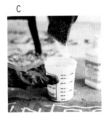 D  E  F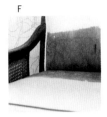

5   The number of times you have to reapply Citristrip depends on how many layers of paint are on the piece. Just keep applying the Citristrip and scraping as you see the bubbled paint loosen until there is no longer any paint left on the wood.

6   When you are sure that all of the paint has been removed, give the
C
D   piece a nice wipe-down with mineral spirits to remove any leftover Citristrip debris and to stop the chemical action of the Citristrip. Be sure you wear the chemical-resistant gloves for this! Work outside or in a well-ventilated area, as the mineral spirits can be a bit strong (even those mineral spirits that are considered "green"). Wear long sleeves to protect your skin. Pour the mineral spirits into a metal or plastic bucket so you can dip your stripping pad right into the bucket and wash the furniture, similar to the way you would wash a car. (Yes, it is very wet and drippy.) The stripping pad really gets into the grooves of the wood and removes all leftover residue and gunk. You may be worried about getting the wood so wet, but mineral spirits are safe to use on all wood and antiques and will not raise the grain or cause the joints to loosen.

7   It may take a few washes to get the piece completely clean. Use fresh mineral spirits and clean stripping pads until all surface residue is gone. Change the mineral spirits solution often to prevent redepositing residue.

8   When you are sure that the piece is completely clean and paint free, allow it to dry for 2 days.

9   When the piece is dry, you can begin sanding with a fine sanding sponge to smooth out and finish the wood.

10   When the sanding is done, vacuum and wipe down the piece with a shop towel to remove any and all sanding dust.

11   Apply the Danish oil directly to the
E   wood with a shop towel, and wipe off any excess with a clean shop towel.

12   At this point, I took the chair to
F   the upholsterer and had him work his magic with our indigo dyed fabric. Lots of hard, hard messy work, but well worth it in the end, wouldn't you say?

APPLYING CHALKBOARD PAINT

MATERIALS

- - - - - - - -

FINE SANDING SPONGE

VACUUM

SHOP TOWELS

DROP CLOTHS

FROGTAPE MULTI-SURFACE TAPE

LATEX PAINT

PURDY 2½-IN/6-CM ANGLED
SASH BRUSH

FROGTAPE DELICATE SURFACE
TAPE

CHALKBOARD PAINT

SQUEEGEE

SMALL ART PAINTBRUSHES (for
cutting in around detail)

PAINT TRAY

FOAM ROLLER

PLASTIC GLOVES

MINWAX SPECIAL WALNUT STAIN

PURDY CHINA SERIES BRUSH

Chalkboard paint has been around for a while now, but I still enjoy coming up with fresh new ways to use it. It's all about the unexpected and quirky. Adding it to a headboard of a traditional bed demonstrates how chalkboard paint can bring fun to any type of piece. I recommend applying chalkboard paint with a foam roller on all of the flat surfaces—this gives a perfectly smooth finish every time.

A

B

C

D
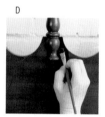

1   Completely hand sand the entire bed frame with a fine sanding sponge. Remove all sanding dust by first vacuuming and then wiping any remaining dust with a damp shop towel. Lay down drop cloths.

2   Use FrogTape Multi-Surface tape
A   to mask off the edge of the area that will be painted with chalkboard paint so that you can paint the bed frame without worrying about getting paint on the headboard.

3   Using the angled sash brush,
B   apply the latex paint to all of the spindles and detail of the bed frame. I use a brush for this because I find that it gives the smoothest finish. "Smack" the brush back and forth (that's really the best descriptive term!) in a quick motion all the way around the spindles. This puts a nice thin

coat of paint on the entire surface and gets into all of the grooves. If the bed you're working on has larger flat surfaces, feel free to use a foam roller.

4   I always apply two coats of paint, so once the first coat of paint is good and dry (about 2 hours), apply a second coat exactly as you did the first coat. Remove the FrogTape as soon as the second coat has been applied; this keeps the lines nice and sharp.

5   Allow the paint to dry overnight,
C   then tape off the headboard edges
D   with FrogTape Delicate Surface so that you can cleanly apply the chalkboard paint. A rule of thumb when applying FrogTape is to use a squeegee to make sure it is completely adhered and nice and flat. If your furniture lines are

see Chalkboard Bed
(page 109)

E

F

G

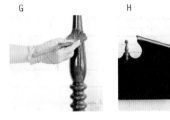

H

straight and you are confident you can keep them straight without using the tape, feel free to do so. I used tape and small art brushes as there was a good bit of detail and a curved edge.

6
E On this flat headboard I used a foam roller to apply the chalkboard paint. Keep the application smooth, being careful not to press down too hard on the roller, which creates lines in your painted surface. Allow the first coat of chalkboard paint to dry.

7 Apply a second coat exactly as you did the first coat. Drying times vary depending on the product, temperature, and environment, so be sure to read the back of the can and follow the directions.

8 Remove the FrogTape as soon as the second coat has been applied. If you leave the tape on too long, it will peel the paint that has gathered at the edge of the tapeline.

9
F I chose to distress the spindles and detail of this bed (only the latex parts, *not* the chalkboard part). Distressing (see page 151) is a preference, not an obligation, so feel free to leave the finish as it is, or sand it and distress it to your liking.

10 When the distressing is done, vacuum the sanding dust off, then wipe the surface down with a clean shop towel.

11
G To complete the distressing, apply Minwax Special Walnut stain finish with a Purdy China Series brush. Cover the entire latex painted surface (*not* the chalkboard paint area) with stain. Apply the stain neatly and smoothly; be careful not to splatter stain on your chalkboard paint surface. Immediately wipe off the excess stain using a clean dry shop towel.

12
H The stain will stay a bit "tacky" for a few days. The chalkboard paint needs 3 days to dry too, so it all works out just perfectly. Both should be dry at the same time, and you can set up your new bed!

CUSTOM PAPER APPLICATION

MATERIALS

- - - - - - - -

VACUUM

FINE SANDING SPONGE

SHOP TOWELS

DROP CLOTHS

LATEX PAINT

PAINT TRAYS

PURDY 2½-IN/6-CM ANGLED
SASH BRUSH

FOAM ROLLER

MAPS (or paper of your
choice)

SCISSORS

MOD PODGE

SQUEEGEE

RULER

CRAFT KNIFE

PURDY CHINA SERIES BRUSH

MINWAX WATER-BASED
POLYURETHANE

For papering this dresser, I was drawn to the muted tones in the map designs by Robbi of the company salt labs. They look like marble to me. Spending some time considering the patterns and laying out how I wanted them to connect together really affected the outcome of this design. Be sure to take time to lay out your designs to see how they intersect and interact the best for the most dramatic result.

A
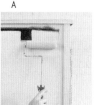

B
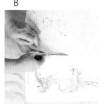

C
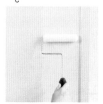

1 Lightly sand, vacuum, and wipe down the entire piece of furniture to prep it for painting. Also, remove the hardware. If you are not keeping the original hardware and need to wood fill and drill new holes, do so now (see page 150). (I chose to keep the original hardware for this piece, so I did not have to do any wood filling.) Lay down drop cloths.

2 Using an angled sash brush and a
A foam roller, paint the entire piece of furniture with a latex paint of your choice; this unifies the surface for the paper application and gives a nice clean base that is not sloppy or unfinished. Allow the piece to dry for 1 to 2 hours. Now you're ready to apply the paper.

3 Start anywhere you wish. For this
B dresser, I started on the side. If you are using wrapping paper or regular maps that you have purchased for your project, just place the paper on the surface you will be applying it to and roughly measure the size you will need. An easy way to do this is to use your fingers to crease where the edges are; then use scissors to cut a bit outside those edges so you have some breathing room. For this specific project, the paper panels were printed by the print-on-demand company Spoonflower.com and were sized to fit the different parts of the dresser. This made my work a bit easier, as I just had to follow the template lines and cut out each section of paper.

see Map-Papered Dresser
(page 117)

D

E

F

G

TIP:

- - - -

Wait to trim all your edges
until the paper is completely
dry. If you try to trim the
paper right after application,
no matter how sharp your knife
is, you will tear the paper,
leaving a messy edge. You will
not be happy about this after
all of your hard work! Be
patient.

4
C When you have your first section measured and cut out, set it aside and roll the Mod Podge directly onto the surface of the furniture, one section at a time, using a foam roller to make sure the application is even and smooth. If the Mod Podge is applied too heavily or unevenly, the paper will bubble.

5
D When the section has been covered with Mod Podge, begin to apply the paper strip. This is where things get tricky. If you are working with wallpaper, it is coated, so you can pick it up and move it around on the surface without its getting damaged. Regular paper is not coated and therefore very thin and porous, so there's no room for error. You must be super careful when applying regular paper—once it sticks to the Mod Podge, it can't be moved without tearing. If the surface you are papering is large, enlist an extra set of hands to hold onto the bottom of the paper and keep it from touching the surface while you work on applying the top.

6 Match up the two top corners and press the top of the paper strip into place. Be very careful to apply it right the first time. Don't rush. When the top has been placed, start working your way down, smoothing with your hands, working from the middle to the edges.

7
E Keep anything wet away from the surface (unless you are using coated wallpaper). Use a dry shop towel to go over the entire paper section you just applied and apply moderate pressure to work out any air bubbles.

8
F When you have done the initial smoothing with a shop towel, go over the entire area with the squeegee. Do not get discouraged if after all of this smoothing you still see small air bubbles. This happens with paper; it is normal! If you have done your smoothing job properly, these will completely disappear when the paper has dried.

9 Move on to the next sections of the paper and apply it exactly as you did in the preceding steps.

10
G When the paper has dried, it is time to trim. Hold your ruler against the straight edge of the furniture and cut the paper between the ruler and the straight edge. Angle the craft knife toward the straight edge of the furniture to keep the paper edge close to the piece. If you hold the craft knife straight up and down, you can end up cutting the paper too far in so it doesn't meet the edge. You do not want any gap between the edge of the paper and the straight edge of the furniture.

CONTINUED . . .

H   I

11 If the drawers are flat-fronted
drawers like in this dresser, the
paper trimming for the drawer
fronts is very easy. Place the
drawer, paper-side down, on a
clean cutting surface and use the
craft knife to trim any paper over-
hang around the edges. I hold onto
the drawer and lean it on the edge
that I am trimming to keep the
craft knife from sliding under the
edge and creating an uneven line.

12 When all of the trimming is done,
H   it is time to seal the paper. When
you are sure your paper application is perfect and dry, it is time
to roll on a coat of Mod Podge. Do
not worry if the Mod Podge creates bubbles in the finish! As long
as you did not have any bubbles
after smoothing and drying, these
new bubbles will go away as the
Mod Podge dries.

13 Sometimes Mod Podge as a
I   topcoat can remain a bit "tacky,"
so I always add a coat of polyurethane over the Mod Podge. Using
a Purdy China Series brush, apply
a coat of Minwax water-based
polyurethane to the entire surface.
Do not overwork the poly—it dries
quickly and will smear and streak
if you keep brushing it over and
over. Allow the first coat to dry
for about 2 hours, then apply the
second and third coats exactly as
you did the first. I like to put three
coats of poly over paper to make
sure it is fully protected.

14 When the last coat of polyurethane has dried, attach the hardware, line the drawers with paper
(see page 152), and fill the drawers
with whatever suits your fancy!

APPLYING WALLPAPER
TO DRAWER FRONTS

MATERIALS

- - - - - - - -

WALLPAPER

SCISSORS

RULER

CRAFT KNIFE

DROP CLOTHS

FOAM ROLLER

PAINT TRAY

MOD PODGE

PAPER TOWELS

SHOP TOWELS

SQUEEGEE

MINWAX WATER-BASED
POLYURETHANE

PURDY CHINA SERIES BRUSH

TIP:

- - - -

These drawers already had a
vintage stain and finish, so all
they required was a quick sanding, vacuuming, and wipe-down.
However, if you are applying
wallpaper to unfinished wood, you
need to first prime and paint
the wood. It is also important
to sand well, making sure the
surface is smooth. If you leave
any surface defects behind, the
wallpaper will shrink right into
them as it dries.

A   B

see Feather Decal Armoire
(page 93)

1 When the drawers are ready, start
planning out how you want the
design to work on the drawer
fronts. It is important to know
exactly where the paper will go,
especially if there is a large pattern
or stripe. Arrange the drawers in
your workspace in the order they
will appear on the finished piece
of furniture. Then, spread your wallpaper out on top of the drawers. I
do this to determine placement and
to be sure the pattern will continue
seamlessly down the drawers.

2 Using scissors, roughly cut out a
piece of paper for each drawer. Cut
generously for this step. Precise
trimming will come later in the
process.

3 Once you have your paper place-
A ment exactly as you want it, crease
off the wallpaper around one
drawer front using your fingers.
Crease around all four sides of the
drawer. The creases will be your
cutting guide. Make sure the crease
marks are visible before you cut.

4 Place your paper on a smooth
clean surface. Use a ruler and craft
knife to cut along the crease lines.
Repeat for all drawers. Lay down
drop cloths.

5 Once the paper for each drawer is
B cut, use a foam roller to apply Mod

Podge to the surface of the drawer
front and the back of the paper.
Use a foam roller to ensure that
the Mod Podge is applied thinly,
smoothly, and evenly. Clumps and
thick streaks will show up in your
paper and cause air bubbles and
difficulty when smoothing.

6 Place your wallpaper on the
drawer surface, being careful to
avoid getting Mod Podge on the
fronts of the paper. Keep lots of
paper towels and shop towels
handy to keep your hands clean.
Smooth the paper with your hands
as much as possible, then use
the squeegee to smooth out and
remove any remaining air bubbles.

7 When all of the paper is in place,
flip the drawer on its front and
trim any excess paper with a sharp
craft knife. Use the wooden part
of the drawer as your guide and let
your knife glide easily against the
drawer sides for a nice clean cut.

8 Use a clean, damp shop cloth to
wipe down the entire surface of
the paper to remove any excess
Mod Podge.

9 Allow the wallpaper to dry completely, then apply two or three
coats of Minwax water-based polyurethane for the protective finish
using a Purdy China Series brush.

PAINTING ON FABRIC

MATERIALS

- - - - - - -

PLIERS (for grabbing onto and removing fabric trim)

CRAFT KNIFE (for cutting and loosening any stubborn fabric trim)

FINE SANDING SPONGES

VACUUM

SHOP TOWELS

DROP CLOTHS

MILK PAINT

PURDY 2½-IN/6-CM ANGLED SASH BRUSH

MINWAX WATER-BASED POLYURETHANE

PURDY CHINA SERIES BRUSH

CANVAS DROP CLOTHS

ACRYLIC FABRIC PAINT

SMALL BOWL OR DISH

ARTIST PAINTBRUSHES (small or large, depending on your design)

STAIN GUARD SPRAY (optional)

I had my old sofa upholstered in canvas drop cloth with the idea to paint directly on the fabric. Canvas has never looked so good; has it? I chose canvas for this project because it is utilitarian, budget friendly, and takes paint really well, but other fabrics can work too. When painting on fabric, use an acrylic fabric paint, and be brave! Spending the money on the upholstery and then painting on it can be nerve-wracking, so take your time and sketch out the design.

A

B

C

D

1
A
Before upholstering, I had to prep and paint the couch frame. When prepping a piece to paint and upholster, it is crucial to completely remove all fabric trim from the wooden surface so that you can paint the entire surface, particularly any trim that butts up next to where you will be painting the trim. It may be tempting to skip this step, as it can take hours (based on how well the previous trim has been applied) and leave you with a few blisters (I should have taken pictures of mine!), but it is a necessity.

2 When you have torn off all of the fabric trim with the pliers and craft knife, lightly sand the entire wooden frame, vacuum to remove the dust, and then wipe down with a dry shop towel to remove any remaining dust. Lay down drop cloths.

3
B
Apply the milk paint to the wooden frame with the angled sash brush. Paint with the direction of the wood grain in nice long, smooth strokes.

4 When the first coat has dried (1 to 2 hours), apply the second coat exactly as you did the first.

5
C
When the second coat has dried, take a fine sanding sponge and lightly distress the painted wooden frame. (This is optional, but I like the look, so I went for it.)

6 When the distressing is to your liking, vacuum and wipe down the entire frame to remove all of the sanding dust.

7
D
When the sanding dust has been removed, apply the polyurethane. Using the Purdy China Series

see Painted Sofa
(page 125)

E

F

G

brush, apply two coats of polyurethane to the entire painted frame, making sure to allow 1 to 2 hours of drying time between coats. Be sure to work in a well-lit area so that you can see the smoothness of your poly application.

8 When the polyurethane has dried, it is ready to be either upholstered by you or taken to a professional. Upholstery is not my gift, so I chose to take my sofa to a professional. I provided three 9-by-12-ft/2.7-by-3.7-m drop cloths to make sure there was plenty of fabric for the job.

9 When the upholstery is to your liking, it's time to paint on the fabric! I have to admit that when my sofa came back from the upholsterer, I was tempted to leave it as it was because it was so clean and beautiful, but I am even more in love with the finished product now. It takes guts to paint on a pretty piece of furniture, but I say go for it.

10 Sketch out and practice your
E designs on paper first before applying them to the fabric on the couch. Upholstery is an investment, and you do not want to take that lightly.

11 Pour some fabric paint into a bowl
F or dish, dip in your paintbrush, and
G paint your design onto the fabric. (I used small artist brushes in this couch design; use whichever brushes best fit your intended design.) Use a moderate, continuous touch so that the flow of the brush stroke remains consistent. It is hard to go back and retrace specific designs, so it is really important to be intentional about the design you are painting.

12 When each painted section is complete, move on to the next section in your design. Follow the design pattern that you created in your sketchpad. It is also good to step back and look at your design as you progress to see if you need to make any adjustments. Work your way around the entire piece of furniture—sides, front, seats, seat backs, and back—until your design is completely finished.

13 Move the couch to a safe, clean place where it can dry for a good 72 hours before anyone sits on it. It is not necessary to seal the painted fabric in any way; fabric paint is intended to be permanent once applied. However, you can choose to apply a stain guard spray to protect the fabric.

In this section, you will find my favorite resources for furniture finds, supplies, home décor, original art, and handmade goods.

FURNITURE FINDS

Daryl Ham, Ham&Sage Vintage

Daryl is the jolliest and kindest hippie soul you will ever meet. He has been collecting interesting and unique finds for years! His vast collection includes lots of mid-century furniture and lighting.

https://www.facebook.com/HamAndSage

Goodwill

Goodwill Industries is always a great source for furniture finds, glassware, and unique vintage items for the home.

www.goodwill.org

Greystone Antiques

My friend Trey owns this local antique shop. Several of the pieces in this book were repaired by Trey and purchased directly from his shop. I tend to buy in bulk from Trey.

www.greystoneantiques.net

Miracle Hill Thrift

Miracle Hill is a chain of nonprofit thrift stores in South Carolina. I find quality furniture and really great glassware and unique vintage furnishings in this store.

www.miraclehill.org

Salvation Army

The Salvation Army is the thrift store where I seem to find the best pieces of furniture, and their prices cannot be beat.

www.salvationarmyusa.org

Screen Door

The Screen Door is one of my favorite places, located in the mountains of North Carolina. It has 25,000 square feet of home and garden accessories from more than 100 vendors and an exciting selection of architectural, antique, mid-century modern, industrial, and country furnishings.

www.screendoorasheville.com

FLOWERS

Whole Foods Market

Whole Foods is a great source for fresh and reasonably priced flowers. I can always find an assortment of pretty blooms here.

www.wholefoodsmarket.com

Willow Florals

Julie Dodds is the owner of this shop in Greenville, South Carolina, and the mastermind behind the gorgeous florals that you see throughout this book. Julie truly has the gift of mixing unexpected textures and flowers together to create stunning visual feasts.

www.willowflorals.com

TOOLS AND MATERIALS

Anthropologie

Anthropologie is a great place to find beautiful hardware. While most people may be headed in to look at the amazing clothes and displays, I make a beeline for the hardware and knobs section! I also sometimes score great rolls of wallpaper here. Find a store near you or order online.

www.anthropologie.com

Benjamin Moore

Benjamin Moore paints are near and dear to my heart, especially the Aura paint line. The colors available are just fantastic, not to mention the paint is smooth, creamy, and never thick. This is my first choice of paint for my furniture projects.

www.benjaminmoore.com

Etsy

Etsy is a great online source for fabric, prints, unique handmade items, home accessories, and vinyl designs.

www.etsy.com

Home Depot

This store is one-stop shopping for all of your furniture makeover needs—paint, tools, supplies, and materials. It is nice to have everything all under one roof, and the prices are reasonable.

www.homedepot.com

Lowes

Lowes is another great hardware store for all of your tools, supplies, paint, and furniture makeover needs.

www.lowes.com

Old-Fashioned Milk Paint

I have used Old-Fashioned Milk Paint in my work since the early 2000s, and I stand behind this product with confidence. In fact, I am so confident in this product that I recently became a retailer! I sell the paint in my brick-and-mortar shop as well as in the Knack online shop. You cannot get the milk paint look with any other paint. If you do not have a local store that carries milk paint, this is the place to get it!

www.milkpaint.com

Salt Labs

Robbi, the designer behind salt labs, collects eighteenth- and nineteenth-century illustrations, maps, and nautical charts, which she reprocesses and incorporates into her designs. She has printed and fabricated a variety of products with these images and crafted a line of home goods with digitally printed textiles and paper. Robbi created the South Carolina coastal maps specifically for the Map-Papered Dresser, page 117.

www.salt-labs.com

Spoonflower

This online shop is an incredible resource for artists and creatives to create and design their own gift wrap, wallpaper, or fabric! Spoonflower does the printing for you. They also offer hundreds of designs if you don't wish to create your own. I use Spoonflower wallpaper and decals in many of my furniture designs and on several of the walls in the rooms in this book. The peel-and-stick wallpaper is easy to apply and removes from the wall with absolutely zero damage or residue. I highly recommend it.

www.spoonflower.com

Suburban Paint

This is my favorite art supply and paint store in Greenville, where I purchase most of my Benjamin Moore paints and all of the Montana Gold spray paint used in my spray-painting projects. It is a family-run business with a super friendly, experienced and talented staff. I am always blown away by the customer service and selection here.

www.suburbanpaintco.com

HOME ACCESSORIES

A Darling Day

Jessica and Neil Barley run this Greenville, South Carolina–based photography and vintage rentals company. Couches, chairs, farm tables, vintage books, collections, china—you name it, they have it. Several props from this company were used for the styling of this book.

www.adarlingday.com

CB2

CB2 is affordable-modern for an apartment, loft, or house and is a sister company to Crate and Barrel and Land of Nod. CB2 always has great finds, particularly unique lighting and accessories.

www.cb2.com

IKEA

IKEA is of my favorite sources for fabric, paper napkins, organizational pieces, lighting, and home accessories. I love the Swedish influence and simplicity in design that is abundant in this store. I used many IKEA pieces in this book, including pillows, napkins, lighting, and rugs.

www.ikea.com

Pottery Barn

Pottery Barn is a great source for furniture, linens, lighting, and rugs. We used Pottery Barn lighting, furniture, rugs, and pillows on pages 78–79, 112, 119, and 128–129 in this book. I love mixing really crisp Pottery Barn pieces with found and eclectic items to create a timeless look.

www.potterybarn.com

Target

Target is a wonderful place to shop for just about anything! I love how Target partners with independent designers to create unique and affordable lines for all. I specifically love the bedding and home décor that Target offers through their Threshold brand. The gold feathers used in the project on page 172 were purchased at Target.

www.target.com

West Elm

West Elm is a national store that presents a beautifully curated line of furniture and home accessories. I appreciate the effort West Elm makes to connect with local artists to create collections of work for their stores. This company is a great example of not replicating art but exalting the creator of the art.

www.westelm.com

ARTISTS AND UNIQUE FINDS

Art & Light

Mid-century lighting, furniture, and artwork are abundant in this fusion gallery run by Teresa Roche. Teresa has an amazing eye for talented artists, and the ever-changing gallery has become a hot spot for local art and emerging talent in Greenville, South Carolina.

www.artandlightgallery.com

Copper & Torch

Lindsay Troutman is the creative mind and pair of soldering hands behind Copper & Torch. Lindsay has been working with glass for over a decade and has a knack for taking something ordinary and flat and shaping it into something functional and beautiful.

www.copperandtorch.com

Cranny + Me

Cranny + Me is a blog and a shop run by my incredibly talented sister, Sarah. I love everything my sister puts her hands to, especially her hand-lettered prints, which can be seen on pages 28 and 32. If you love beautiful Instagram feeds, my sister has one of the prettiest, sweetest, and most inspiring ones around! Follow her: @crannyandme.

www.crannyandme.com

Crave Studio

Jennifer Bedenbaugh is the maker and creator behind this gorgeous line of ceramics for the garden and home. I personally own several pieces of Jennifer's and sell her work at Knack as well. Jennifer made the ceramic pinch bowls on pages 88 and 102–103.

www. crave-studio.com

Emily Jeffords

Emily Jeffords is an impressionistic landscape painter working in oil on canvas, creating artwork for collectors around the world, and collaborating with select brands. The gorgeous paintings on pages 96–97 were created by Emily. Much of her work is centered on the theme of finding peace and beauty, regardless of life's challenges.

www.emilyjeffords.com

Everly Lane

This lovely Etsy shop is full of beautiful and shiny paper garlands! These talented makers made the garland around the fireplace mantel on pages 130–131.

www.etsy.com/shop/EverlyLaneDesign

Ink Meets Paper

The sweetest husband-and-wife creative team are behind this really wonderful paper line. Each product created supports their belief in the handwritten and the handcrafted. The 100-percent cotton paper is thick, and the ink is mixed by hand. Each piece is printed one color at a time on an antique printing press in sunny South Carolina.

www.inkmeetspaper.com

Joseph Bradley Studio

Joey's use of color is fantastic, and the beauty and softness of his paintings are wonderful. I love how Joey uses lots of metal leafing in his work as well as the animal life theme in most of his paintings. The yellow bird, koi, and fox paintings seen on pages 68, 70–71, 73, and 86–87 were done by Joey.

www.josephbradleystudio.com

Koelle Art

Annie Koelle creates beautiful paintings of birds, bugs, and landscapes, as well as geographic prints. One reason I am so drawn to Annie's work is her use of found frames and objects to create the backdrop for her light and airy work. The couch project on pages 124 and 182 was created by Annie as well as the gold illustrated walls and owl painting in the foyer on pages 104–105.

www.anniekoelle.com

Lily Pottery

Enter a Lily Pottery shop and be prepared to want everything there! Treat yourself to handcrafted ceramic and metal jewelry designed in-house, as well as an amazing collection of vintage furniture, housewares, boots, and accessories. They have an online shop as well for those of you not in the area!

www.lilypottery.com

Milk Moon

Angie Thompson's hand-lettering skills, shibori-dyeing skills, art, creativity, and all around awesomeness are seen on many pages of this book, from her shibori pillows on pages 126–127 to the constellation chalkboard on page 127, as well as the artwork on pages 64–65 and 80–81. Follow her artistic endeavors on Instagram: @milk_moon

www.MilkMoonblog.blogspot.com

Olive and Grey

Keith and Tanya Leland are a talented husband-and-wife team who design and paint signage. Several of these signs can be seen in this book on pages 66, 81, 92, and 98.

Palmetto Home and Garden 2
422 Laurens Road
Greenville, South Carolina

Royal Buffet

An Etsy shop offering intricate and beautiful paper work designed and created by artist Mollie Greene. The dream catcher and word banner used on pages 43 and 90 are just a small sampling of the beauty found in this shop.

www.etsy.com/shop/royalbuffet

Shinola

Shinola is a local hot spot for treasure seekers and junk enthusiasts alike. Anyone who has found treasures at Shinola (and there are many, including me!) know it is worth the trip every time. Rugs, artwork, lighting, pillows, and knick-knacks from this amazing place are used in the styling of this book.

19 Mohawk Drive
Greenville, South Carolina

ARTIST CREDITS

Kent Ambler, pages 90–91, 106–107
Laura Baisden, pages 90–91
Mandy Blankenship, pages 90–91
Victoria Elizondo, page 54
Joe Engle, pages 122–123
Finkelsteins Creature, pages 90–91
Paul Flint, page 67
Stephen Freedman, pages 122–123
Katie Wuthrich Gerdt, pages 88–89
Corey Godbey, pages 28, 32–33
Kirsten Hansen, pages 92, 98
Hannah Rael Hawk, page 24
Oh Albatross, pages 122–123
Chris Stoffel Overvoorde, pages 122–123
Pixels & Wood, pages 90–91
Shannon Plourde, pages 106–107
Beth Schiable, pages 122–123
Angie Schmerbeck, page 24
Turning South, Marvin Payne, pages 122–123
Chanee Vijay Textiles, page 115
Joyce Stratton, page 95
Vitrified Studio, page 115
Katie Walker, pages 67, 122–123
Whiskey & Honey, page 115
Harrell Whittington, pages 34, 78

To the One whose breath fills my lungs and moves me to create, I praise you.

To my husband and best friend, I love you and am so thankful that you are my life partner. Your tireless support of all of my endeavors has inspired me to press on and do my very best. Thank you.

To my beautiful children, whom I love deeply and who are so very important and special to me. You are the greatest treasures I have ever been given.

To my mom and dad, who have supported, encouraged, and cheered me on the entire way: I love you and am so thankful for all you have taught me. Mom, thank you for exemplifying such hospitality in our home and for teaching me to collect and gather things that I love.

To my brothers and sister, thank you for always calling to catch up on the latest, and for caring about my passion and work. I love you guys!

To the Knack team that helped make this book a reality and a pleasure: Jessica Barley, Angie Thompson, Julie Dodds, and Paige French. Each one of you has enough talent in your little finger to change the world, and I am so thankful that we got to work together on this project. Each of you gave 100 percent for every single shoot, behind the scenes and beyond, and I could not have asked for a better crew. You are "the dream team."

To Neal Barley of Thoroughfare, for providing us with delicious and sustaining food during several of our photo shoots.

To Dan Hamilton of Hamilton and Company, for letting me borrow your big bad box truck! I absolutely could not have completed the many photo shoots without your generous loan.

To Michael and Shinola Antiques, for letting us fill our cars with styling props and goodness from your shop. This book would be missing a good bit of character without our finds from Shinola.

To all of my lovely friends who opened up their homes and studios for this project. Cory and Erin Godbey, Chris and Annie Koelle, Lily Wikoff, Teresa Roche, Emily Jeffords, Joey and Rachel Bradley, Craig and Jennifer Bedenbaugh, Neil and Jessica Barley, Andrew and Lib Ramos, White Whale Studios, Art & Light, and Mike and Audra Erkens: Thank you for sharing your beautiful spaces with us and for generously giving of your time so that we could capture all of the gorgeous photographs that fill this book. Your homes and studios are truly inspiring and perfect examples of living with what you love.

To all of my readers, friends, and supporters, thank you so much for the constant excitement and encouragement you gave throughout this entire project. The power of your words was such a positive and motivating force for me.

To my editor, Laura Lee Mattingly: Thank you for always being on top of your game and for not ever cutting corners or rushing things. Your attention to detail and your focus on the project makes magic happen. Thank you for always being there to talk to when things got scary and for your excellent leadership.

To my copy editor, Kristi Hein, managing editor, Sara Golski, and proofreader, Ellen Wheat, thank you for your tireless and perfect efforts to make this project correct in every way. I admire your gifts. To the rest of the Chronicle Books team—in particular Allison Weiner, Yolanda Cazares, and Stephanie Wong—thanks for all you did to help bring this book to life.

To my agent, Stefanie: Thank you for always looking out for my best interests and for being so encouraging about every project that comes my way. You are a wonderful and knowledgeable friend and colleague.

To Hillary Caudle: Thank you for two beautiful book designs. You rock!

"The Dream Team" (L to R): Jessica Barley, Angie Thompson, Barb Blair, Julie Dodds, Paige French.